"[Weekly Writes] was such an encouragement to me. The prompts gave me great ideas and really made me do some deep thinking about a great variety of subjects and topics. I would definitely take this workshop again and again since it was those prompts that kept me wanting to write daily and write more." - Val Gordon (British Columbia, Canada)

"[Weekly Writes] was truly a gift during a time when that creative spark was seemingly gone. I printed out each prompt and inserted it into a binder with blank pages. At the end of the program, I had a complete writer's journal to look back upon each time I needed that extra boost." - Jennifer Hollowell (Livermore Falls, Maine), Owner, J.M.H. Creative Solutions (http://jmhcreativesolutions.com)

"Shery Ma Belle Arrieta has given me a gift that will never get dull, wear out or stop giving. Through Weekly Writes she has given me the place to start, the courage to do it and the encouragement and knowledge that I can be a writer or anything else I choose to be. Thanks, Shery, for designing, producing and writing Weekly Writes. I highly recommend this book to all authors. Newbie or pro – you will gain something from it. Guaranteed." - Billie A. Williams (Amberg, Wisconsin) Author of Writing Wide and mystery suspense novels Death by Candlelight, Tung Umolomo and Fire at Thunder Ridge (http://www.billiewilliams.com)

"Weekly Writes provided [me with] the necessary discipline that every writer requires…[and] the modules were great fun to do." - Mary Attard (Malta)

"I received Weekly Writes during a low point in my life. [Weekly Writes] gave me an outlet to vent feelings and learn to cope with those feelings. I would recommend Weekly Writes to everyone. Even if you have no desire to be a writer, you will learn a lot about yourself doing each assignment."
- Helen Fields (High Point, North Carolina)

"I have thoroughly enjoyed the diverse activities and suggestions in Weekly Writes: 52 Weeks of Writing Bliss! After a long day at work as I sit in front of my laptop, I often find stimulating subject matter evading me. Fortunately, the suggested exercises in the Weekly Writes have helped me to chip away at the spindly legs of that cumbersome pest called Writer's Block. Not only do I have exciting topics to write about, I continue to gain strategies for creating my own alluring writing ideas. Weekly Writes has proven to be a valuable source of motivation to improve my writing. So, as I learn, my students learn." - Linnel Little (Jacksonville, Florida)

"The Weekly Writes modules have given me lots of ideas in toying with various aspects of the human emotion. By doing the exercises, anyone can come up with so many ideas to do when writing." - Alexa Villano (Quezon City, Philippines)

"I'm a teacher, a mom, a wife, leader of a writer's group and find myself really pressed for time. Sometimes it's just easier to not write even though I know I need to. Weekly Writes was perfect for me: I knew that I would write because the prompts were there waiting for me. It was easy, effective, and challenging." - Dawn Allen (Olathe, Kansas)

"As a published author, I value the fifty-two gems of wisdom encompassed by the fifty-two weeks of Weekly Writes. Each of them, studied in no particular order, is of value to any writer. They stir the 'little gray cells' to invoke the muse and seriously approach a word processor. I have enjoyed and do enjoy this tutelage on the craft of writing. Bravo!" - Bob Howard (Lakeview, Oregon)

"[Weekly Writes] is truly excellent. The prompts encourage you to plumb the depths of your memories and experiences to come up with writing that is both unique to you and universal to the human condition. A winning combination, if ever there was one." - Manjul Bajaj (New Delhi, India)

# WEEKLY WRITES:
# 52 Weeks of Writing Bliss!

## by

## Shery Ma Belle Arrieta

ISBN: 0-9710796-7-6
Library of Congress Control Number: 2003115962

First Edition

Published by Filbert Publishing, Box 326, Kandiyohi, Mn, 56251, USA.

Manufactured in the United States of America.

# WEEKLY WRITES:

# 52 Weeks of Writing Bliss!

## by

## Shery Ma Belle Arrieta

Weekly Writes: 52 Weeks of Writing Bliss!

# How to Use this Book

This book is designed to keep you writing for fifty-two consecutive weeks – one whole year. The writing activities are short and approximately take five to twenty minutes of writing time every day.

It is best to start Weekly Writes on a Monday, and tackle one prompt each day. When you are done with one writing activity, do not proceed to the next one right away. Come back to this book after twenty-four hours and then do the next one.

Tackle the writing activities in the book this way and you will be able to develop the habit of writing regularly no matter what mood you are in.

Selected chapters include examples by writers who have taken the e-mail workshop version of this book. The examples you will read are rough drafts or first drafts.

Additionally, a section of this book contains 100 writing prompts and ideas. These prompts were generated by **WriteSparks!™**, a software I created for writers. Information on how you can download this software is included in this section.

I hope you experience writing bliss with the help of this book. I would love to hear all about it so do e-mail me! Have fun writing!

Shery Ma Belle Arrieta, Author
E-mail: **writershery@ewritersplace.com**
Web site: **http://ewritersplace.com**

# Week One: Twists

This week, you will experiment with different endings, and you will take your cue from the movies you have seen.

First, pick a movie. Any movie will do. Next, in your notebook, write a summary of the movie. Keep this under three paragraphs. Below the summary, describe the ending or the final scene.

When you work with the prompts in this book, do not stop to edit your work. Write as fast as you can and simply let yourself go. You can have a go at this in two ways:

1. Set a timer for say, five minutes, and then write everything that comes to mind based on the prompt and stop when the five minutes are up.
2. Write for as long as you can and when you are tired or have filled an entire page, stop.

Now you are ready to write...

Monday: Today is Science Fiction day.

Re-read the ending or final scene of the movie you picked then re-write it by giving it a Sci-Fi twist. Think Star Trek, Matrix or Men in Black.

Be descriptive. Do not be limited to the movie's plot. Add a character or an event. Be creative. Give your imagination free rein.

Tomorrow, you will use the same ending and give it another twist.

Tuesday: Tuesday is Drama day. Re-write the ending of the same movie by giving it a dramatic twist. Make your ending as emotionally charged as you can make it.

Wednesday: Wednesday is Horror/Suspense day. Re-write the ending of the same movie by giving it a horror twist. Scare yourself.

Thursday: Thursday is Romance day. Re-write the ending of the movie by giving it a romantic twist. Make your characters fall in love. Be as cheesy and sappy as you want.

Friday: Friday is Adventure day. Re-write the ending of the movie by giving it an adventure twist. Think Indiana Jones or The Mummy.

Hannibal has set the table and made preparations for the dinner with Clarice. Paul is tied up and drugged, spouting babble as he watched Hannibal sauté the mushrooms with fine wine. These complete, Hannibal sets them aside and turns to the main dish: Paul. Hannibal knows a lot about Paul from his meticulous research—but also by the mere fact that he had been living here in Paul's cabin for several weeks.

Not even sure what's happening, Paul keeps babbling as Hannibal busies himself cutting open Paul's brain. As the blades of the Stryker saw cut through the skull, the saw suddenly hits something metal and stops! Cursing, Hannibal peers down to see what's keeping the blade from its work. Seeing metal, he assumes it's a plate and casually asks Paul if he was perhaps a veteran. Not understanding Paul's incoherent response,

Hannibal decides to cut around that part. Finished with all but the one area of the skull, he pulls an instrument from his medical bag and chips away the last part very gently.

During the "surgery," Hannibal notices that only a small amount of blood is dripping from the makeshift cap and as he lifts it off Paul's head, he could see why. Paul's brain is made entirely of electronic components—it's a computer! Stunned, Hannibal steps back and as he did so, Paul's eyes turn red. With an unexpected strength and swiftness, Paul breaks free from his bindings and lunges at Lechter.

Upstairs, Clarice is putting on makeup and fixing her hair, not sure why this felt so important to her. In fact, she can't remember much about her life before these hazy weeks in the cabin. However, she does know that Hannibal is her savior and the center of her life at this time. His gentle care of her had eased her pain over these weeks and even the pain stemming from her childhood. She finds him charming and quite funny as well. Not only that, but Hannibal is an excellent chef, as evidenced now by the odors wafting from the kitchen to her room. She feels grateful to Hannibal and pleasing him tonight is her only focus, and focus is hard to come by for Clarice these days.

Downstairs, she hears a loud thump and wonders what Hannibal is up to. What could be the disturbance? Not feeling panicked or even upset, just mildly curious, Clarice walks downstairs and saunters to the kitchen. It is empty. Didn't she hear voices earlier? Stepping in a little bit closer, she notices the back door swinging open in the wind. She peers outside. The only movement is the gentle sway of the weeping willow as the wind tickles its branches; the only sound is the music of nature on an early summer day by the ocean.

Out of the corner of her eye, she sees movement. She turns to look. She finds herself staring into the crimson eyes of Paul. How did she know his name is Paul? Before she could figure it out, he reaches for her and pulls her into his arms.

"Are you all right, Clarice?" His voice sounds oddly mechanical.

"Where's Hannibal?" she asks.

"The monster is dead," says Paul and he begins to steer her back into the house.

"Dead? But we're supposed to have dinner tonight," she murmurs. Her head feels foggy and she desperately wants to lie down for a nap. "Paul, I'm so tired."

"Yes, I know. You've been through a lot. Let's get you back to the city where you can be plugged in and recharged."

# Week Two: Sovereign

The New International Webster's Dictionary defines sovereign as:

1. having undisputed rights to make decisions and act accordingly;

2. having unlimited, absolute power [over something]

This week, you are the King or the Queen of your own world. You control everything and you have power over all things.

Power comes with responsibility, though, so every decision is not just something you make based on a whim.

<u>Monday and Tuesday</u>: You have recently inherited an island from a distant relative. The fun part is that you can bring people with you to populate the island. However, you can bring only 21 people.

Who will they be?
What are their areas of expertise?
What can they do?
How old are they?

This is like the biblical Noah's Ark, but instead of choosing pairs of animals, you are choosing the kind of people you need to be with you in your island.

So go ahead, make a list of 21 people you want to bring with you. They do not have to have names while you create your list. Create fictional people or people based on your ideals. Give them occupations, personalities and quirks.

Next, create a short profile for each person on your list. This time, give each person a name. Your profiles can be one or two paragraphs. Get to know your people.

<u>Wednesday</u>: Last Monday and yesterday, you created 21 profiles of the 21 people you intend to bring with you to your island.

Today, you are going to convince these people to come with you. What is in store for them? Why would they want to go with you?

So imagine yourself in front of your chosen 21. You have their undivided attention. You need to make that one great speech, and if there ever was a perfect time to deliver it, it is now.

Be persuasive. Market your island. Make your speech so great, none of your chosen 21 will ever want to be left behind.

<u>Thursday</u>: If you are going to own an island, govern it and lead 21 people, you have to have rules in place. These rules will (hopefully) keep things in order in your island.

For ten minutes, jot down rules or laws everyone in the island must follow. Hey, your rules do not have to be conventional. Remember you are the boss so you can be creative with your rules or laws!

When you are done, go over your list of rules and choose one. Visualize yourself explaining to your chosen 21. Make them see the importance of this rule. Do this for 10 minutes.

<u>Friday</u>: Freewrite for ten minutes using "power" as your focus word. What is power to you?

Here is an activity to tide you over the weekend:

Choose one person or two (or more) from your profile list. Write a short story about her. Make her the 'star' of her own story. Perhaps a monologue of someone who is about to leave behind everything in order to come to the island. What is going on in her mind? How does she feel about starting all over again?

**Father John Bowsley,** Ordained Minister, 42. Father John believes in non-denominational religious practices and is willing to conduct services in a different faith each week. He will also run the Sunday school for the children when the need arises.

**Knowla Henderson,** Supreme Court Judge, 44. Knowla has sat as a judge for the past 15 years and is very well respected, fair and equitable. Knowla brings with her a wealth of judicial knowledge that we can use to establish our governing system on the island.

**Mary Jane Wilkens,** Government Purchasing Agent, 35. Mary Jane is a logical choice because we will need to have access to many products at a reasonable price if we wish to establish a market economy on the island.

**Letta Markus,** Chartered Accountant, 28. Letta is smart as a whip when it comes to financial decisions. She will make sure our market economy, having a solid investment strategy, flourishes.

**Leland Miller,** Disk Jockey, 41. Leland, rated as the world's number one disk jockey for the past seven years, will be an asset as he is very entertaining. He will be functional in establishing our tourism industry – dancers, performers, actors – while keeping the islanders entertained (mainly, of course, the ladies).

**Franklin Dejong,** Entrepreneur (Northwest Cruise Lines), 45. Franklin has a world of experience in the tourism industry, having run cruise liners for the past twenty years. He will be an asset in establishing our transportation to and from the island as well as our gambling and entertainment business. He will assist John West with the accommodation end of the business.

**John West,** Architect/Building Engineer, 30. John will be responsible for designing and overseeing the building of every structure on the island. He will create both public and private habitats, as well as simple outdoor structures, such as public restrooms, creative and useful artistic elements, and distinct landmarks, which will make our island unique.

**Marcus Longlimbs,** Investment Banker, 55. Marcus will be essential in obtaining financing for our development from his many rich business clients and investment personnel at various large corporations through sponsorship, advertisement, and development projects that will pay huge dividends. He will also open our island, once developed, onto the New York Stock Exchange.

**Marianne Mercer,** Chief of Staff, Mercer Hospital, 30. Marianne is renown for the medical breakthroughs at many of her hospitals on the mainland. She will be beneficial in establishing an excellent medical facility on the island to treat our guests and residents when needed.

**Liddia Langley,** Surgeon, General Practice, 27. Liddia is well known as an excellent surgeon at Marianne Mercer's Boston Hospital. Before becoming a surgeon, Liddia was a general practitioner. Therefore, she will be able to cope with everyday illnesses and meet the needs of the more seriously ill at the same time.

**James Queens,** Electrician/Instrument Mechanic, 31. James is a good looking, top of his class, electrician with a background in instrumentation, which we will be able to use in every facility on the island. His background includes electrical, plumbing, gas fitting, and electronics, but he also has experience in various other trades, which will serve the island well.

**Katey Carpenter,** Interior Designer, 23. At the young age of 20, Katey has already established herself as a world-class interior designer, and has since designed residences and business establishments all over the world for the rich and famous. Her specialty is making things look expensive for very little money, which is why she has made it to the top so quickly.

**Marcie North,** Master Chef, 33. Marcie opened a chain of restaurants a few years ago that has become very chic. The restaurants are a hit with everyone as they serve superb food, following in detail Marcie's recipes, and are reasonably priced so that the common man can enjoy them as well.

**Henry Lakeside,** General Contractor, 35. Henry has overseen many building projects and has gained an international reputation for bringing a project, big or small, in on time and on budget. He will oversee all aspects of the buildings as well as staffing.

**Nancy Wilcock,** Public Relations Executive Secretary, 28. Nancy will be responsible for all documentation on the island and scheduling and itineraries for all personnel as well. Nancy will deal with every aspect of public relations and media relations, which is her specialty.

**Julie Dwight,** Hair Stylist/Beautician, 24. Julie is a leading hairstylist and beautician in New York City. She will fit in well on our island. As an entrepreneur, she will be able to add additional information to our tourist industry requirements – especially from a feminine viewpoint.

**Tim Bechary,** General Laborer, 29. Tim has worked in many fields and has vast experiences that will add to our growing population. He is fun loving and good-natured.

**Glenda Jackson,** General Laborer, 23. Glenda has worked in every field, from chambermaid to waitress. She has a wonderful sense of humour, but a temper to match her red hair. She will add a certain spark to the island's population.

**Jeremy Philips,** General Laborer, 35. Jeremy holds a degree in law and security, but has not used it in many years. Here on the island, he will work as a general laborer, jack-of-all-trades, until we are established and then he will take over as the chief security officer.

**Nathan Wilson,** General Laborer, 28. Nathan's background is in carpentry, but he has also worked in the entertainment industry as a bouncer. Although he is large, his temperament is one of a gentle giant. He has a thing for red heads.

**Jeff Bridges,** General Laborer, 31. Jeff is a teacher by trade, but has worked in several other trades over the years, including plumbing, carpentry, millwright, etc. He will run the local school once our island is established.

The great speech:

Hi Everyone,

Well, by now you are asking yourselves why I invited you here. The truth is that I want you, my friends, to be in on the ground floor of something positively wonderful. I am offering you a solid investment in your future and something that will bring you an insurmountable amount of pride and satisfaction.

As you may remember, last month, I inherited an island from my grandmother. The island is uninhabited and as such belongs to the United States, but has not, as of yet, become an independent country. What I am proposing we do, and please hear me out before making comments or asking questions, is to set up and run a world-class tourism industry on this island. You may have noticed I have been very selective of those I have asked to join me. Each of you has a specialty that will enhance the island's prospects. Each of you will also contribute to the others' economic survival, as well as the islands.

My grandmother also left me a tidy some of money, which will sustain us while we build our masterpiece, but we will require additional revenue to build our homes, condos, tourism facilities and that is where you come in. Before making our way to the island, each of us needs to raise as much capital as possible to invest. The return on the money will come in the form of percentage of ownership. For each dollar you invest or your clients invest, you will receive one share of the ownership. I, too, will be on equal footing and have already had the island appraised at fair market value. Your return will be twofold. You will receive your share's return on every dollar of profit made, plus you will have a say in establishing a place like nowhere else in this world.

I know this is asking you to take a big step away from your current life, but everyone here is single and performs a specific function required on the island. I have one other incentive to offer each of you. A life in paradise, so how could you possibly refuse?

Okay, now I will entertain your questions and discuss your specific function on the island and at the end of this question period, we will see who is with us.

(Three hours later, it became apparent that many of these individuals definitely were interested. To my surprise, when I asked for a decision at the end of the meeting, only one individual was undecided. I pondered replacing the person, but before I could decide my course of action, that person joined in as well. Now all we had to do was raise the funds necessary and build it.)

Rules of the island

A list of rules and regulations:

1. Everyone must marry someone from the island within the first year of being there – myself included.
2. Divorce is forbidden; therefore we offer family counseling services for free.
3. Everyone will have a say in every decision made, but majority will rule, and with twenty-one people there will never be a tie, which means I will not vote, as owner.
4. All children born on the island will attend church and school on the island until the completion of their high school education. Jeff will take correspondence school to upgrade his high school teaching requirements. Upon completing high school, the children are free to leave the island for higher education, which we will pay for on the condition they return to the island as a permanent resident and practice their craft – no matter what it is. If they do not wish to return to the island, their parents will pay their educational fees from their portion of the profits.

5. Rules from the basic charter of rights and freedoms will be observed here, with the exception of the above rules.

My idea of rule number one: I feel that if everyone marries someone from the island, the likelihood of them leaving the project lessens by half, and when the children come along, it lessens by even a great amount. You will note, with the inclusion of myself, a female, the number of males and females are equal; therefore providing a partner for each person. This is an insurance policy, which will be enforced by rules number 2 and 3. Father John will upgrade his counseling services through correspondence school, until electrical hook up is complete and then he will finish his studies using television learning and the Internet.

The meaning of power

Power to me is an optional word, which, in this instance, I have used to seduce people into traveling to the island with the understanding that they have equal say in all matters related to the effective construction and operation of a major tourist function. This power structure puts everyone on equal footing, making it possible for a craftsman to marry a Supreme Court judge and feel that they weld the same amount of power. It thereby takes the sting of position out of the equation and makes it a more harmonious situation for all involved.

By granting equal power, you not only encourage and build on the strengths and weaknesses found in each individual, but you also establish a new set of rules, which in itself allows for self–governing and little or no law enforcement requirements. By using this method, each individual involved retains his or her structure and status as part of the pride of the community, and as such, would not want to fall down in anyone's viewpoint, and especially not in their spouses. By adding the children to the equation, this strengthens the unions and sets a moral standard for all to follow and exemplify to visiting tourists and their own children.

Another profile:

The person I have chosen to profile is myself, as I have not been introduced into the equation:

**Trish McQueen,** Con Artist, 26. I am feisty, athletic, and a likable individual. I am an open-minded, free spirit who believes in the impossible. I have always taken from the rich and given to the poor. As a professional con artist, I have spent my life, to date, making people believe I can do the impossible, with a little help and financial contributions from them. To date, my criminal record reads like the who's who in the society column of the local newspaper. So as you see, this situation is no different from any other situation I have created in the past, except that this time, I have full intentions of going straight. Unless of course, this endeavor fails, at which time, I shall be sailing somewhere in sunny Florida with a rich widower in tow. ;-)

# Week Three: Bounties

<u>Monday</u>: Recall a time when a stranger showed you generosity. Where did it happen? What did he do or give you? How did you feel? Freewrite for ten minutes.

If you have not experienced this yet, then recall a time when you showed generosity to a stranger.

<u>Tuesday</u>: The ideal writer. You know this writer exists and you want to meet her so you can pick her brain. Problem is, this writer is nowhere to be found.

Create the profile of your ideal writer.

- What does the ideal writer look like to you?
- What does she write?
- What is her typical day like?
- What is her personality?

At the end of your profile, include your bounty -- the reward you are willing to give to anyone who finds your ideal writer.

<u>Wednesday</u>: Whenever I finish writing something, I reward myself. It can be watching a movie on CD; taking a long, hot shower; buying/reading a new book; anything that will make me feel good about myself. Something that says, "You did a good job today, Shery."

What "rewards" have you given yourself lately? Write about these rewards.

<u>Thursday</u>: Ever heard of the communication theory, Pavlov's Classical Conditioning? It involves a dog and a bell.

In a nutshell, when the bell rings, the dog salivates. The dog associates the ringing bell with hunger and food. The bell, in this case, is a stimulus for the dog's reaction.

Although today's activity does not involve bells, dogs or saliva, it does involve your own conditioning to writing.

What is your writing stimulus?

<u>Friday</u>: Do an online search for two or three publications you want to be published in. Copy and/or print their submission guidelines.

If the publication has an online version, explore it. Read the articles; learn from other writers; get a feel of the publication's style.

Now, imagine you see your byline there. What is your story about? What is your style? Why do you think the editor accepted and published your story? Freewrite for five minutes.

You do not know it, but at the end of five minutes and you look at what you have written, you will see a rough draft of a query. It is up to you if you are going to follow through with it and get your reward – publication.

Foggy mornings. Hiding, changing the real world into a dream-like state. Daring you to imagine what may be lurking in the shadow of the bush over there, or the muffled sound from over there. Walking in the quiet morning fog the only sound the swish, swish of my jogging suit that doesn't jog but merely walks those 10 or 20 minutes stolen from my day. "Too early," sings the black capped chickadee that wrote my haiku poem.

A misty river, calm, serene, staring up at cloudless lavender and pink morning dawn. Calm the surface, but not the tide/the current deep beneath the placid state. Its poetry hangs imbedded in a message not yet delivered and I dare to dream.

Was it a quote that stirred my muse that sent the ink spewing from my pen. The quotes always seem to come from some directed hand that knows my mood and what I need to hear. H.G. Wells, "If you are in difficulties with a book, try the element of surprise: attack it at an hour when it isn't expecting it." Good advice when I needed it that day. I unstuck me at 4 a.m. that next day.

Or this morning's quote by Aristotle, "To write well express yourself like common people, but think like a wise man." Ah, the brilliance of those quoted folks, they get my pen to move.

Anytime I read or re-read Natalie Goldberg, any of her books, I must, there is no way to refuse. I must write. She unlocks the words and magically they flow without opening a vein from my heart, mind and soul. I write.

Try one more – just discovered joy. Write Sparks. A treasure trove of magic words to start my magic carpet ride with pen in hand.

Weekly Writes: 52 Weeks of Writing Bliss!

28

# Week Four: Lessons

The most effective lessons we learn are the ones we carry with us for life. They shape us into who we are and are often instrumental in future decisions.

Monday and Tuesday: *Lessons from Home*: Recall the time when you were between the ages of 13-19, and you lived with your parents and siblings (if you had brothers or sisters). For three minutes each, freewrite on the following:

- a lesson your mother taught you
- a lesson your father taught you
- a lesson your brother/sister taught you
- a lesson your aunt/uncle taught you
- a lesson your grandfather/grandmother taught you

Wednesday: *Lessons from Friendship*: On our journey through life, we meet many people. We make friends and form bonds with people who share our interests, values, and beliefs. We become friends with those who might be quite the opposite of who we are. And sometimes, we lose them too.

Friends do come and go, but there are friends who stay with us all through our lives. The friendship we have with them lasts a lifetime. And there are friendships that have great impact on our lives, even though they last only for a short while.

Think of the very first best friend you had and for ten minutes, jot down the "lessons" your best friend unknowingly taught you. Based on the lessons you come up with, write a thank-you letter to your best friend.

<u>Thursday</u>: *Lessons from Love*: Has your life become fuller and more meaningful all because your spouse or partner loves you? How has being in a relationship helped you become a better and a more mature person? Freewrite for ten minutes and then write a thank-you letter to your spouse, partner or special someone.

<u>Friday</u>: *Lessons from Life*: For fifteen minutes, freewrite by starting with the phrase, "My experiences have taught me many important things, and one of them is..."

All my life I have wanted to find one best friend. Someone I could share my life with and someone who would accept me and my iniquities. The person should be someone I could be comfortable with.

I finished high school without finding that one person. I showed a bit of myself to close friends but not all of me to one person. I remember praying for this one great gift during my teen years.

And just when I stopped praying and just when I was too busy with my studies to think about building friendships, she came. She came all too naturally. I was in college then, in a school that was not as friendly as the school I had previously come from. This school was in the city, and I was faced with a different culture and different folk.

This girl was my classmate in only one subject. I noticed her because she had the most fashionable bags and wore a new blouse or shirt every day. She was silent but she always found time to say pleasant things to me. I ignored her. I was such a snob in college.

30

The lessons I learned from her: 1) it pays to be friendly; 2) there is no harm in baring your soul to someone; 3) a friend is a stranger you still haven't met; 4) families are important in life; and 5) going to mass each day could take the blues away.


Dearest Ivy,

We have been friends for decades yet in each turn and twist of my life, you have always been the dear friend that I know, always supportive, always there. You also let me feel that I am needed all the time and that I have a reason for staying alive.

Things are different for us now. We each have our own lives to live. I hardly ever see you nor talk to you, but I still feel that you are there whenever I need you.

Thank you so much for being the friend that you are. Thank you for the lessons learned and for accepting me as I am. I am sure that wherever life may lead me, in all my successes and failures, you will always be a part of every joy and every tear.

Good luck.

# Week Five: Seasons

My country, the Philippines, is a tropical country and has only two seasons – the wet season and the dry season. Countries like the US and Canada have several – winter, spring, summer and fall.

Seasons come and go, and then they come again. It is an unending loop.

Here are your writing activities this week.

Monday: Associate a season with a smell and freewrite for ten to fifteen minutes. Craft a poem, an essay or a story that starts with the smell you associate a season with your season.

Tuesday: Associate a season with an emotion or mood and freewrite for ten to fifteen minutes. Craft a poem, an essay or a story that starts with the emotion you associate a season with.

Wednesday: Associate a season with a color and freewrite for ten to fifteen minutes. Craft a poem, essay or a story that starts with the color you associate a season with your season.

Thursday: Associate a season with a symbol and freewrite for ten to fifteen minutes. Craft a poem, an essay or a story that starts with the symbol you associate a season with your season.

Friday: Associate a season with a family event or experience. Freewrite for ten to fifteen minutes.

A suggestion: Try each prompt for every season (e.g. associate winter, summer, spring and fall with a smell) and freewrite separately.

Green: all the varied shades of green that belong to spring. The bright and cheery frog green of Spring peepers, or the tiny brilliant emerald green snake hiding under my day lilies.

The lush and varied green of the northern Wisconsin forests in spring – olive green, sage green, emerald green, pea green, chartreuse green, yellow green, blue-green. They are all there in all the hues no man can imitate. Spring green renewal, re-growth, richness. No wonder paper money is green.

No wonder the passion of jealousy is green.

The moss green, the mildew green of a stagnant pond is not dull in spring, nothing is dull in spring.

Kermit the frog says, "It ain't easy being green," ah, but dear Sesame Street frog you're envied for your green. The ivy green, the emerald Isle green of Ireland the shamrock green spring tide ocean-green, so many greens. Shades of each other but never the same greenness.

If I were green, I would be the muted green, sage like green, of the north side of a tree—moss green.

Spring green in variegations of the Hosta plant leaves, spring is all greenness and all greenness is spring.

# Week Six: Spaces

<u>Monday</u>: Take a blank sheet of paper. Draw a circle in the middle and write "space" inside the circle. What do you associate with the word "space"? What does the word make you think of? Put each word, phrase or concept, inside a circle.

If you come up with five words associated with "space" then you have five circles surrounding the first circle. Connect those circles to the first circle. Next, look at the words in your outer circle. What are words you associate with them? Repeat the process by putting the words in their own circle. Do this for ten minutes.

What you just did is called "webbing" – a creative writing technique. By webbing, you are branching ideas and finding relationships among them.

Look at the page you filled with words you associate with "space." Pick one or two words/phrases/concepts and freewrite for ten minutes.

<u>Tuesday</u>: One meaning of "space" is "the distance between two points or objects." Think of someone you know. What is the space you two have, physically and emotionally? Write for ten minutes.

<u>Wednesday</u>: Freewrite for ten minutes by starting with the phrase "My eyes scanned the wide open space and I felt..."

<u>Thursday</u>: Imagine yourself inside a box that is just big enough to let you move around but not bend. It is dark and hot inside. You look up and you see there is a hole, big enough that one of your fingers can fit in it.

35

Describe what could be waiting for you outside the box. Do this for five minutes.

<u>Friday</u>: Go back to the webbing activity you did last Monday. Take out this page and look over the words you associated with "space." Pick out five to eight of the words in your web and use all of them in a poem, story or essay.

Psychologists use the words "Personal Space" -- like don't stand too close to me. I like my space. Your nearness makes me uncomfortable. I start to think. Do I smell fresh and clean, is my deodorant working, does my breath smell of last night's pizza. All these space things, but when you were tiny, just fresh from the womb, your baby powder pink sweetness, ah those nestled moments when you breast fed—no danger, no space between us.

And as you grew, our space did too. Friends, school, life pushed and shoved between us. We allowed it to push. Then came boyfriends, marriage, they were your life. The space grew and grew. Grandchildren pulled the space and shrunk it gradually again until we were at the point where we knew nothing else but mother and daughter and new life to love. Then your process started with the three you grew and nurtured. We disagreed at some frivolous point, but you withdrew and pushed. A steel plate between us grew, between my life and you. Sometimes I catch a glimpse over the top of, around or through that impenetrable wall you've barricaded you with and it since has grown to encompass all that touches you and never me.

Tears won't melt it down, letters, phone calls, pleas only stare back unanswered from my space outside your wall.

What more can follow and will you come when the pastor says "ashes to ashes dust to dust," will I look down from heaven high and see one tear grace your eye? Or when the lawyer calls to say "last will and testament will be read today," will you then take down that wall?

Will the wall shatter then and our spaces close again or will...

# Week Seven: Meanings

This week, you will only do one kind of writing activity. You will repeat this process every day. At the end of the week, you will have five different essays, stories or poems.

The tools you need? An old (or new) dictionary, notebook and pen.

<u>Monday, Tuesday, Wednesday, Thursday and Friday</u>: Grab your dictionary, open it on any page and point to any word at random. Do not read the definition of the word. If it is a word whose meaning you already know, try another word. Write the word down in your journal or notebook. Create your own meaning of the word. On gut feeling, what does the word make you think of?

Here is an example:

"Coruscate" makes me think of snowflakes in my hands… it's the feeling I get when I rub them against my palms...

Continue writing about the image or feeling you visualized from the word.

Notice your focus is not on the word anymore, but on the image or feeling that resulted from the word.

(If you want to look up the meaning of the word, go ahead. It is not important in this activity, though, because we merely used that word to jumpstart your writing.)

When the ten minutes are up, look over what you have written and see if you can polish it into a poem, story or essay.

I chose the word "Rigmarole" from the dictionary for this exercise. To me, this word sounds like it is describing the motion waves make as they crash to the shore, when they roll and toss and twist and turn towards the shore and then crash to the beach.

And after I got this image in my head and wrote for a bit, I came up with a little poem about it.

The Waves

At the beach
With waters wide
And crystal clear
The waves do ride
From out beyond
They twist and roll
Coming in
To break the lull.

They wash to shore
And crash and foam
To end their journey;
They know it's home.
Then still waters
On the sand do stay
Before more waves
Are on their way.

# Week Eight: Creations

Welcome to another week of Weekly Writes. The prompts this week are short questions, and it is up to you how you will answer them. Be creative and just let your imagination fly...

<u>Monday</u>: What can you create out of a shoe box?

<u>Tuesday</u>: How can you make a matchbox fly?

<u>Wednesday</u>: What can you create out of empty pens?

<u>Thursday</u>: What can you create out of old videotapes?

<u>Friday</u>: What can you create out of several decks of cards?

# Week Nine: Solutions

Brainstorming is a creative problem solving tool. When brainstorming, you are not required to come up with purely logical ideas or solutions.

When you are given a prompt question that needs to be addressed, you give solutions to it no matter how weird or wild these solutions are.

Brainstorming helps you come up with out-of-the-box ideas you can use to jumpstart your creative pieces.

For your writing activities this week, you will brainstorm ideas to use in your stories, essays or poems.

Below is a list of 'problems' for you to solve. Brainstorm and create a list of solutions for each problem. Solutions do not have to be logical or rational.

Monday: Someone sent you a box full of unused stamps. What are things you can stick stamps on (except letters)?

Tuesday: You have a chessboard but the chess pieces are missing. What can you use?

Wednesday: How do you open a jammed door?

Thursday: How do you fix a picture frame that keeps falling off the wall?

Friday: What are paper clips good for (aside from holding paper together)?

My former college roommate sent me a shoebox full of unused stamps for my birthday. I guess she remembered my stamp collection that I kept in a box in our dorm room. Of course, none of these new stamps fit in the old album. And, she made a stupid rule that I couldn't use them on any letters. "Be creative," she wrote.

I set some on the piano to use as stickers during lessons for students who practiced this week. Students who memorized their pieces can take enough to decorate their folders since school is about to start.

I culled all the pinks, blues and yellows. Pasted them to the living room lampshade. Covered it entirely. Nice eclectic effect. Used red and green stamps to replace the magnets on the refrigerator.

Later when I was scrapbooking, I selected stamps with people on them. I smiled smugly as I covered the faces of people I didn't like. Just as much fun as cutting them out of the pictures.

I still have enough stamps left to create a collage. I've seen posters of stamps pasted together to create another image. Gave that a try and am satisfied with the result. Created a 25-cent LOVE stamp like the ones we both used on our wedding invitations in 1989. I shipped the resulting stamp "art" back to my college roommate. My rule: You must hang this in a prominent place in your home!

# Week Ten: Baggage

What do you think a person named "Joe Smith" looks like? For me, he is an average guy with a kind face. He is probably between 5'7" and 5'10, and he has plain, brown eyes. He works as a plumber and has a wife and two kids. He is a likable guy, so he has a lot of customers. I could go on about what he likes to do or how he dresses... all that by just by looking at his name.

This week, you will do what I did. You will create personalities around names. You will give them a life, and you will explore the baggage they bring with them.

Baggage? Yes, baggage. Have you ever wondered what other people put inside their baggage? Just how many clothes they bring for a two-day trip, or what kind of toiletries they bring? Then there is the 'emotional baggage' – the kind of baggage they bring with them wherever they go.

Below are names:

- Hillary Brown
- Elsa Heidenberger
- Klaus Muller
- Jennifer Thomas
- Lucius Kramer
- Mary Louise Anderson
- Aaron Gergye
- Maria Garcia
- Stephanie Wilson
- Jeremy Banks

Your job is to create personalities for each person.

What do they look like?
Where were they born?
What are their professions?
What do they like?
What do they hate?
Do they have families?
Are they married?
How old are they?

Look at their names and simply go with your instincts. Create personalities for each of them based on how you perceive their names.

Next, put each person in an airport. They are all going someplace. Where would a person with the name Jennifer Thomas be going? What could an Aaron Gergye be doing in an airport? And what could be in their baggage?

Lastly, what 'emotional' baggage could a Hillary Brown or Lucius Kramer be carrying?

You have ten names with ten baggage to write about this week. Work on two names per day.

**Hillary Brown**: She's 5'6", with green eyes and blonde hair. She's a middle-aged lawyer and mother of two boys. She was too busy that she didn't even go to her eldest son's wedding.

**Elsa Heidenberger**: She's an average single woman in her 30s, brunette, 20 lbs. overweight, 5'7" and an accountant in a decent law firm. Mrs. Brown is her boss' associate. Elsa is a bit introverted.

**Klaus Muller**: He's in his early 30s, 5'10" and of average build. He is happily married and a father to a 4-year-old girl. He works as a janitor in an airport and even though he earns meager wage, his family lives decently enough.

**Jennifer Thomas**: She's a high school cheerleader and she graduates this year. She's 19, tall, pretty with blonde hair and blue eyes. Her father's a rich businessman and urging her to go to Harvard. However, she couldn't bear to tell him she didn't make it.

**Lucius Kramer**: He's a 24-year-old writer. He was called a geek back in high school because he used to wear thick prescription glasses. He transformed from geek to a stud after college. He's about 6'1", with a solid build, dark hair and brown eyes. He is a photographer for a magazine.

**Mary Louise Anderson**: She's a 10-year-old patient. She's blind and can't walk on her own because of a disease she had when she was a baby.

**Aaron Gergye**: He's 5'10" and average looking. He's the nurse assigned to take care of Mary. He's 23, a new graduate and a bit nervous on his first job.

**Maria Garcia**: She's 38, 5'4", brown skinned, black hair and has brown eyes. She's a Filipina working as an airport staff.

**Stephanie Wilson**: She's 29 years old and mother of two boys and a girl. She's a typical mom, but she's divorced.

**Jeremy Banks**: He's almost six feet tall, in his early 30's, with black hair and a funny mustache. He's one of the police assigned as an airport security officer.

Glaciers (an excerpt)

I thought it was just another typical snowstorm. I still went to that old airport to get some pictures. I brought along a thick coat, my 'survival kit' and a flashlight. As I drove, the storm got stronger. The road was blocked. The local airport was about two blocks away so I left my car and walked the rest of the way. When I reached the airport, I saw the huge sign, "Merry Christmas and a Happy New Year."

"Merry Christmas?" I asked to myself. What's merry with this Christmas? It's just a hollow, commercialized holiday used by businessmen to lure people into buying their merchandise.

When I entered, it felt warm. The heater was working well. I took of my coat and left it in the baggage counter. In the arrival area, I waited as if I was waiting for someone. I was waiting for the plane to arrive so I can observe how the people around me would react upon seeing their 'loved ones' coming home for Christmas. An hour passed, and the plane arrived with three hundred fifty passengers. It was the perfect opportunity…

As my camera flashed, the lights in the airport went out. Screams were heard everywhere. People panicked. After 15 seconds, the emergency lights turned on. From a lively airport, the place turned into a dark chaotic pit. The emergency lock had closed the doors and we were stuck inside. I hid the camera in my bag and sat silently on the floor. The place was too dark to walk around.

I tried to relax. I heard someone praying beside me. For me, they only prayed because they were afraid to die in this cold and lonely place. If I were to die at that point, I couldn't have cared less.

Then I heard two children crying. With all the commotion,

why was I able to hear them? I ignored them, but something inside me told me to go and find the children. When I reached them, I saw a toddler and a small young girl in a wheelchair.

"Tasukete... Tasukete..." the toddler cried.

"What?" I asked.

"She's crying for help," the young girl said.

I wondered who the young girl was. She looked about nine years old and she wore a funny hat. The toddler wore bunny pajamas.

"So, how can I help you?"

"Mister... we're cold and we're hungry," the young girl cried.

"I'm sorry, I can't help you with that."

The young girl hugged the toddler and said, "Dai jo bu yo, Tomoyo chan..." (We'll be alright, Tomoyo.)

I couldn't bear to leave those two alone. I held the handles of the wheelchair and pushed. The toddler sat on the young girl's lap.

"Where are we going?" she asked.

"Don't worry, I know this place like the back of my hand." We stopped at the abandoned snack station.

"This place is so empty."

"Most of the passengers were advised to go to the conference hall," I said. I looked around and saw vending machines. They varied from the ones that contained toiletries to ones that served coffee. I left the two kids by the chairs. I walked around looking for the right machine to knock down.

Then I saw the ones that contained chocolate bars and juices. I grabbed a steel chair and bashed the vending machines with it.

"What the heck are you doing?" I turned around. It was just the janitor.

"Um… we're hungry," I said.

"Oh," he said as if nothing happened. "Why did you ruin the machines like that? Don't you know I don't have my cleaning equipment with me?"

"I'm so sorry… I guess."

He grabbed a chocolate bar and said, "Those two youngsters are waiting for you there."

"Okay." I went to them. I handed them the snacks and said nothing.

"Mister…" the young girl was holding a bar of chocolate.

"What now?"

"Have some, it's good."

The janitor came to us and said, "Well, hello there, young ladies."

"Hi, mister..."

"Just call me Klaus."

"What are you three doing here, why didn't you go to the conference room like everyone else?"

"We're lost..." the young girl said.

"Oh, really?"

"It's so dark that little Tomoyo here got scared."

"Tomoyo, that's a name you wouldn't normally hear," Klaus said.

"Her parents are both Japanese and they were on vacation here for two weeks," explained the young girl.

"So, where are her parents?" Klaus asked.

"We lost them along with Aaron..."

"Aaron?"

"He's my personal nurse. He was going to take me to the hos... to my home, yeah, to my home to celebrate Christmas."

"How did you freaking meet this kid?" I asked rudely.

"Well, I met her parents on the plane," the young girl answered.

"So you two are looking for your parents, right?" Klaus asked.

"Yes sir."

"Poor kids. If it weren't for this blasted snowstorm, I would be home with my wife and my daughter this Christmas Eve."

"I'm so sorry."

"Don't be, young lady."

Klaus went to get his flashlight. When he came back, he flicked it on and aimed it at a picture on his wallet.

"This is my wife, Julia, with my kid, Stacy."

"Oh, both of them are so pretty," said the young girl.

"You haven't told me your name yet," said Klaus.

"I'm Mary Louise Anderson. You can call me Mary, Mr. Klaus."

"Nice to meet you then Mary, and you too, young Tomoyo."

Tomoyo just smiled.

"She's aloof around strangers."

"Hmm, so who's that guy with you?"

"I don't know. He doesn't talk much."

"Hey, you there. Kindly tell these ladies who you are at least..."

"Lucius..."

"Lucifer?" Mary and Klaus asked in unison.

"It's Lucius, stupid!"

Klaus laughed at me. "You're a hothead. I remember you. You're that social pervert who takes pictures here every week!"

"What? I am no social pervert, I'm a photographer!"

"You're that 'dreamy' boy those ladies have been talking about."

"What ladies?"

"You're quite famous with the ladies here, y'know," Klaus said.

I didn't answer. Klaus' two-way radio rang. "I should be on my way now," he told us.

Weekly Writes: 52 Weeks of Writing Bliss!

# Week Eleven: Wrappings

The ways we "wrap" ourselves give other people different perceptions or impressions that are very different from who or what we really are.

In high school, I avoided wearing skirts and girl clothes. I was shy but I hid it behind a glower and eyebrows that constantly threatened to fuse. My "touch-me-not/scary wrapping" cost me a few friends.

In college, I wore shirts and plain, faded jeans that were full of holes. And sneakers. No girl shoes for me. I wore black lipstick and black nail polish; my hair had violet streaks -- it practically killed whatever hair follicles were left on my father's head. And I managed to scare a few of my Nepalese and Thai classmates, thanks to my "weird wrapping."

When I started working, corporate suits replaced the shirts and jeans, and high-heeled shoes took over my sneakers. Suddenly I was a 22-year old adult dealing with government people, giving them instructions on what to do – all because I had a "corporate wrapping."

Most of the time, people relate to us by how we come across to them, by how we are "wrapped."

The following are questions for you to ponder and write about this week, and you guessed it... it is all about "wrappings."

As usual, spend at least ten to fifteen minutes freewriting.

<u>Monday</u>: What is the one thing you most want to have? If someone is to give it to you as a surprise gift, how should he

wrap it? How big a box should it come in? What should the wrapper look like?

Tuesday: What is your usual attire when you go out? Are you a jeans-and-shirt person? a skirt-and-blouse? From a stranger's perspective, describe yourself when you are seen in public places.

Wednesday: Take out those photo albums and look at old photos. Find two or three people and describe how they looked. What 'wrappings' did they come in back then?

Thursday: What was the best gift you have ever received? Do you remember what the wrapping it came in looked like?

Friday: Spend a few minutes people-gazing. Simply look at people. Note the ones that catch your interest. What did they look like? How did they dress? What were their most distinguishable characteristics?

# Week Twelve: Detours

A detour is a deviation from a usual pattern or course; a path taken to avoid an obstacle or danger; a longer route taken in order to get to a destination.

<u>Monday and Tuesday</u>: Name a place that is about fifteen to twenty minutes drive from your home. What things are between your home and that place? Shops? Parks? Libraries? Cafes?

First, imagine yourself going home from that place. Write a direct and 'un-detoured' description of your drive home. Do this for five minutes.

Next, imagine yourself again going home from that place. This time, describe the things you will see along the way, and the 'detours' you might take before you actually pull up to your driveway.

Will you stop at the grocery?
Spend a few minutes sipping coffee in a diner?
Stop and chat for a while with someone you know?

Write for ten minutes.

<u>Wednesday</u>: Recall a time you avoided someone.

Why did you avoid that person?
What measures did you take to avoid him?
How long did you avoid him?
Was there a confrontation?

Write for ten minutes.

Thursday: Someone from your past calls you and tells you she wants to visit you. You could not say no. This person is not someone you are entirely fond of so you want to delay her arrival. She asks for directions to your home. What is the longest route to your place? And who is this person? Why are you not keen to see her?

Friday: Someone from your past calls you and tells you he wants to visit you. You could not say no because this person is someone you were very fond of and you had spent many great times with him. He asks for directions to your home. What is the shortest route to your place? And who is this person? Why could you not wait to see him again?

Here are additional ideas for this week's theme. Start your freewrite sessions with the help of the phrases below.

- Before I go to bed every night, I...
- One of the things I want to do is _____ but I haven't done it yet because...
- I wish there's a way to get to _____ more quickly...
- I avoid eating _____ because...


Fear


As the sky changes from azure, to vermilion, to black, I remain immobile. Cars have come and gone. Various groups of people scuffled past me. Some in silent groups, some in lonely solos and most, lost in a roll of laughter. I envy them. When was the last time I ever laughed? I take a long drag from the menthol cigarette in my hand.

I squint my eyes. They sting. Curses! I wish they would not sting as much. Lately, though, they have been stinging like hell. I wish they'd just dry out so they won't hurt anymore. I stare at the star-filled sky. I imagine one stretching its arm towards me; I feel the warmth of its blinding light around me, casting me into limbo. I wish with all my might that I could just disappear with them as dawn comes. I wish never to hear one more cock crow. Never to see another ray of sun. Never to come home and risk seeing the inevitable.

If I could just stay here forever. Anywhere, as a matter of fact, except home. As the night deepens and begins to cast its icy winds about me, I know I must go. The stars will not fetch me tonight. Right now, I will have to make do with a few hours of tranquility. I take another slow drag and finally stomp what remains of my seventh cigarette to the ground. I sling my backpack on my shoulder and begin my lone trek home.

The air grows heavier and thicker as I near the doorstep. Despite the well-lit front yard, this house has always been dark. "Lay-off the lights! They're perfect. It's not them, it's you." I quoted some pathetic break-up line. Back in my carefree days, I'd have laughed at that cliche. But tonight, I'm not laughing.

I hurriedly make my way up the endless flight of stairs to my room. Carefully avoiding any soul or I'll be forced to establish eye contact. They're too intimate. Pierces right through your soul. I hate them. With a thief's stealth, I was able to make it past the other doors to the security of my room. The only place where I can stop smiling for everybody's benefit. I don't really like smiling.

Inside the dark room, light seeps from beneath the closed door at the opposite side of my bed. This leads to the bathroom. I know I shouldn't, but I couldn't prevent my feet from drawing near. I turn the cold knob. Latch clicks. I make my way through. And soon, these noises inside my head. Heart and mind talk too much. I don't know whom to listen to anymore. They will not be silenced.

"You can't run away forever. Delay it now, it will be there tomorrow." Heart.

"And what? Risk getting hurt? Spare yourself the pain." Mind.

"Save yourself. Go inside." Heart.

"Save yourself. Turn back." Mind

I take a deep breath and slide inside. Head turned towards the floor, hands behind my back; I lean against the door behind me. There is no turning back.

I draw steadily nearer, breathing a heavy sigh I square my shoulders to face her and saw in an instant that which I feared most. She is an empty shell.

Clenched jaw. Knitted brows. Eyes burning through me. Daring me to probe deeper. I did. There is anger. Emptiness. There is pain. So much sadness. She trembles. A child whose innocence has been corrupted. She hungers for understanding---and forgiveness.

Youth was a crime. She believed the world could be trusted. She was wrong. She was young. He was a married senior officer. She was an idealistic grad. She trusted his good intentions. He only saw her flesh. In one dreadful night, innocence was shattered.

She was forced; she had to tell the truth. But nobody understood. Truth is not a juicy gossip. She endured the public's hits and blows with downcast eyes and silence. She was filth.

Now I ask the heavens for forgiveness for I cannot find purpose in my existence. As I look at my reflection in the mirror, I understood that this is the truth that I have been avoiding. I am but a husk.

But something burns from behind that gaze. I cannot tell... it seems to be a flicker of hope. Could it be possible that I still believe? I drop my gaze. A small smile creeps across my face. The sun will soon rise.

Weekly Writes: 52 Weeks of Writing Bliss!

# Week Thirteen: Loopholes

A loophole is a way of evading a situation, rule, contract or law.

This week, you only have one writing assignment: Write a contract between you and your Writing Muse (or Creative Side or Creator)

The contract should address the following:

- What are the things you expect from your Muse?
- What are the things your Muse can expect from you?
- What courses of action will you take if/when your Muse does not 'deliver' at some point?
- What courses of action will you take if/when you do not live up to any one of your Muse's expectations?
- How are you and your Muse going to work together?

As you create your contract, think of any loopholes that may arise. Address these loopholes in the contract and give alternate courses of action.

Take your time creating this contract. It might take you several drafts before you arrive at the final version.

What do you do when you finish it? Print it, sign it and keep it near you to remind you what you need to do.

Weekly Writes: 52 Weeks of Writing Bliss!

# Week Fourteen: Indecision

Indecision oftentimes hinders us from achieving goals we have set for ourselves. Indecision can cause regrets. How many times have you said to yourself, "If only I..." or "I wish I had..." or "If I only did it another way, then..."

Where there is indecision, there is no resolution. Instead of being convicted to a decision, a stand or a principle, indecision causes us to 'swing' from one side to the other; to take one step forward only to take two steps back.

Indecision breeds reluctance. And where there is reluctance, there is a certain fear -- fear of trying, fear of doing, fear of failing and yes, even fear of succeeding.

This week, you will come face to face with your indecision.

Freewrite for ten to fifteen minutes. Based on your freewrite, go on and craft an essay, story or poem.

Monday: Think of something you wanted to do last week but did not do.

What was it?
Why did you not act on it?
What hindered you from doing it?
How do you feel about not being able to do what you wanted?

Tuesday: Now think of something you wanted to do last week and you went ahead and did it.

What was it?

Why did you act on it?
How did you feel after doing it?

<u>Wednesday and Thursday</u>: Freewrite using any or all of these prompts:

- I remember ten years ago when I _____, and if I can do it all over again, I would...
- One of the things I regret not doing is...
- One of the best decisions I've made is...

<u>Friday</u>: Brainstorm and list at least five situations you hope you never have to find yourself in. Then, write the courses of action you would take if you do find yourself in those situations.

One of the best decisions, which I can say I have so courageously achieved, was leaving my job in the city and going back home. I look back now and appreciate how much courage I had then and I still thank God for such courage because no one was there for me then except Him.

When I graduated from high school, I went to the city to study. After passing the board exams, I joined the corporate world. For three years each, I worked in a bank. My rise to the ranks was rather exceptional mainly because I chose to tread the road less traveled. In my third year at both banks, the great feeling of going back home always bothered me.

Home is the province where my family is. Home is a place where there are no big malls, no big stores, no nightspots and fewer opportunities. Home is simply the place where I belong.

My first attempt at trying to go back home proved to be immature. I quit my job, I went home and floated around. Before that year ended though, I received an offer from another bank in the same city where I used to work so I went back. There was no question about it because I enjoyed my work. However, the nagging feeling of leaving everything was always there. It always happened between my second and third year on the job.

When I worked in the city, my salary was good enough to make me and my siblings live comfortably and enjoy city life. I did enjoy. I went out a lot, enjoyed bars and everything there was to go to. I lived comfortably and had many friends to help me through. Most of all, the job required me to travel a lot; it was another opportunity worth taking.

Then my third year on the job arrived, and along with it was the nagging feeling. This time, the feeling pushed me to the brim. So I mastered enough courage and quit work. My friends and family thought I had gone crazy. Anyone in her right mind would have traded places with me and there I was giving it all up. And where did I go after? Home. No job and not a promise for one and no business either. What I brought home with me were the experiences and the memories and the strong feeling of just going home.

My family was not at all happy with my decision. I was going to be an intruder to their already well arranged life. My transfer meant using my room, and some people moving out. It was not going to bring good to anyone and they thought it was not going to bring good to me. Never have I felt unwelcome in my entire life. They did not help me. I was the only one who packed and shipped ten years of accumulated memories from my city life. And the packed things remained in our garage for months.

The inner strength was always there and it stayed there at times I was too idle to think straight. Nobody spoke to me at home, but I had to stand by my decision. Of course, there were days I wanted to run and go back to the city but there was always that courage that pulled me up. Soon I was offered a job and things started to lighten up.

As the years go by, the more I am able to appreciate the courage I had then. For me, going back home was one of the best decisions I ever made.

# Week Fifteen: Reactions

Newton's Third Law of Motion: For every action there is an equal and opposite reaction.

This week, you will be writing about your reactions. Spend ten to fifteen minutes every day freewriting on each prompt.

Monday: Turn on the radio or TV and listen to any news station. Watch out for news items that catch your attention. Listen to the news carefully. Afterwards, turn off the radio or TV and begin writing about your reaction to the news you have heard or seen.

Tuesday: Take out your favorite newspaper or magazine and read it. Pay attention to stories that catch your interest. What were you feeling as you read the stories? How did you feel after reading? Write your reaction.

Wednesday: Someone you have never gotten along with for years suddenly steps up and says hello to you while you are walking in the park, shopping or having coffee in a diner. She strikes up a conversation as if the two of you are the best of friends. How would you react?

Thursday: You are in a bookstore and you happen to 'bump' into your favorite author (or personality). Who is he and what is the first thing you will say to him?

Friday: You are walking in a public place. After a while, you notice that people are looking at you very oddly. What could be causing them to look at you that way?

A release from the prison of the unconscious. What must it be like to come out of a coma after 19 years? Is it like waking up from a long dream?

Denial. This just cannot be. The changes in the world are surreal. Maybe the dream continues--how else can he explain where he is right at this moment? The last thing he remembers clearly is driving with his friend. Dead? How can his friend be dead? Somebody wake me from this dream, please! I cannot move--my body is foreign to me. Familiar faces, but different-- older. Aged overnight. Strangers, doctors, media. People have lived their entire lives from beginning to end--inside the space of my coma.

Confusion.

Just Yesterday

Where am I?
I don't recognize this place.
Sterile, cold, loud and busy.
How can anyone sleep in a hospital?
Just yesterday I was home...
Please wake me up!

Why am I here?
I can't remember anything.
Fear grips me.
Mom, Dad...what happened to you?
Your faces--instantly older.
Just yesterday you were young...

Where is my daughter? I ask the woman.
Vaguely familiar...
"It's me," says she.

I can't understand this.
Just yesterday--an infant

What do you mean Fred is dead?
I saw him just yesterday.
Help me because I can't wake up--
This has to be a dream.
Everything is so strange.
Just yesterday the world made sense.

Cars--those are cars?
Strange shapes--tail lights,
concept cars--must be
a big auto show...
What happened to my K car?

I set the alarm and hope it works
To wake me from this nightmare
The alarm clock sounds
I'm...not waking up.

Is this life a gift?
Let me go back to sleep--
when I wake, it might be
Just yesterday again.

(Background: I heard the tail end of a news story on the radio about a man who came out of a coma after 19 years. Here's some info about it: http://www.newarkadvocate.com/news/stories/20030721/opinion/618282.html. I "reacted" to it because of my own experience of having a closed-head injury, being in a coma and waking up a week later in the hospital not remembering what happened or how I got there. I truly believed I was having a very irritating nightmare until about two weeks after I was home. The funny/weird part is that I kept trying to figure out how to wake myself up from this "nightmare" because I could not understand/accept that I wasn't dreaming. How must the guy in the news story have felt after 19 years?)

# Week Sixteen: Peaks

Monday: Make a list of the high and low points in your life. You can categorize them by year, phase (e.g., childhood, teens, adult), or event (e.g., marriage, career, special occasions).

If it would help if you add short descriptions to each of those, do so. However, do not write about any of them yet. Just list them all down first.

Today is your brainstorming day.

Tuesday, Wednesday, Thursday and Friday: Look at your list and pick one high point from each category (e.g., childhood high point, teen high point and adult high point.)

In the next four days, write about your chosen high points. Spend at least 10 minutes freewriting on each point. If you want to freewrite about the other highs, do so.

Weekly Writes: 52 Weeks of Writing Bliss!

# Week Seventeen: Word Strings

Word stringing is a technique you can use to generate ideas for your stories. You begin with a word and the object is for you to come up with a new word that begins with the last letter of the previous word. You do this until you have generated at least ten words.

The words need not be related because word stringing is done quickly and automatically.

For example, the word is JOB. A word string for it might be something like this:

job branch hospital legal left trial letter reliable envious serious sweet trustworthy youthful

Use the words to guide you when you freewrite or when you want to begin a story.

This week, create word strings from the following list of words, and use the words you generate in a poem, essay or story.

Monday:
- amazement
- remembrance
- county
- change

Tuesday:
- bloom
- August

- admonish
- eruption

Wednesday:
- unwieldy
- genie
- diary
- diploma

Thursday:
- silence
- impending
- oasis
- reflex

Friday:
- whistle
- prosper
- hangar
- boundary

Word string for Silence: silence, eerie, early, year, redeem, memories, strength, hands, stolen, never, ready

Sitting in the early morning silence, eerie memories crept into my mind. The strength of the memories from that day, ten years ago, gripped at me like hands around my neck.

Word string for Diary: diary, yell, lies, stars, steps, straight, tears, strong, girl, lonely, yellow, why

"Leave me alone!" the girl yelled as she ran up the steps to her room. She went straight for her diary. Its pages already so full of her tears, she turned to a blank page and began to write. She wrote about being lonely and of lies.

# Week Eighteen: Wallpaper

<u>Monday and Tuesday</u>: If you were wallpaper,
- what color would you be?
- what design, motif or pattern would you have?
- what room or wall would you cover?
- what kind of person would pick you?

<u>Wednesday</u>: Using the word stringing technique you learned last week, make "wallpaper" your first word. Generate at least 10 more words then use all the words in a poem, a story or an essay.

<u>Thursday</u>: Is your room covered with wallpaper or paint? If it is covered with wallpaper, describe the wallpaper in detail. If it is covered with paint, what is the color and how does the color make you feel in general?

<u>Friday</u>: Write about a typical day in your room (or any other room in your house). Write not from your point of view, but from your wall's point of view. You can take this activity further by writing from the point of view of the fan standing in the corner of your room or from the point of view of the most worn-out book in your bookshelf.

There's this kid who lives in my room. This kid's a bit untidy. Every time he arrives from school, he rushes towards my room and leaves everything on the floor.

He leaves his dirty clothes, his pasty polo shirt and faded dark pants on the bed. He leaves his CD player and all its wires hanging.

79

He leaves his books on the floor. He throws his smelly shoes at my face.

Little did this kid know about my existence. I'm always in his room, watching him every time he is studying; every time he writes some weird short stories; every time he listens to his CD player and his annoying music; every time he stares at me and ponders about what would life bring him. What would his future be like? What will he be as a person?

I notice this kid is quite the loner. Maybe company abandons him. Maybe it's him who abandons company. Maybe it's just me. I'm always in this room and I don't know what happens to him every time he's outside.

In fact, he doesn't stay here that much. He's always out or in front of the PC in the living room. He doesn't get to stay much with me except when he sleeps. I've been with him for almost two years since they moved here, yet I don't know him. Maybe most of his relationships work that way.

# Week Nineteen: Visions

Your writing activities this week are based on the five different meanings of the word "vision."

1.  someone or something beautiful and delightful;
2.  a dream, fantasy, inspired revelation;
3.  a product of one's imagination; imaginary thing;
4.  foresight; ability to anticipate and prepare for future events;
5.  insight

Monday: Who (or what) is the most beautiful person (or thing) you have seen? What makes this person/thing beautiful? Freewrite for ten minutes.

Tuesday: Describe one of your most recent dreams. Recall the details of your dream. What do you think was the dream trying to tell you? Explore and write about it for ten minutes.

Wednesday: Children have great imagination. They make up stories and even imaginary friends. What stories did you invent when you were a child? Did you ever have an imaginary friend? Write about it for ten minutes.

Thursday: How do you envision yourself five years from now? Ten years from now? Fifteen years from now? Twenty years from now? Where would you be? What would you have accomplished? Freewrite for ten to fifteen minutes.

Friday: Make a list of topics or issues you feel strongly about. Choose one from your list and explore it. Write about what you think and how you feel about your chosen topic.

Imagination helped me grow. It still does. I have my heart at doing creative things from the days I remember well. I was five years old when the first incident happened. My parents felt I drew well so they took me for a painting competition.

The competition was for children in the 5-10 age group. I was the youngest and a first-timer. The function was organised at a government school in Trivandrum City. I knew what I was to draw. There was no theme. I drew the "Backwaters of Kerala" – a man rowing a small boat full of coconuts through the backwaters. Surprisingly, I came out the winner. I was given the first prize. It was my first endeavor, first success story, a beginning for the many prizes to come in the next few years. I was proud of with my achievement.

When few similar successes followed, I started dreaming, dreaming of a life as an artist. My auntie was an artist. If she could draw portraits so well, even of those people she has never seen, why couldn't I be an artist, or paint a portrait? My parents encouraged me. I still remember those moments when I waited during the school assembly for the school principal to announce my name. I could walk up the stage with pride. Those days, when every time, the whole school heard only of "Resmi Shaji" as the artist so often. I would dream of how I would grow up as writer. I spent a lot of time dreaming about my artistic love, drawing in my rough books during free class periods, intervals, without even going out to play.

I had the power to dream; because I believed I was successful as a child, no one could ever say my paintings weren't up to the mark for a child of my age. People, too, declared I would grow up to be an artist. Hence, there was confidence within the self, encouragement and support, especially from my parents and also, from my teachers and classmates.

To hear my name being announced in many competitions, including those at the national, state and regional levels always made me feel proud. I trusted there was some great power within me. Something, which could let my imagination turn true. Imagining myself being one of the world's best and well-known painters! I am glad after a break of more 12 years, I am again tuning myself to be an artist!

Weekly Writes: 52 Weeks of Writing Bliss!

# Week Twenty: Steadfastness

To be steadfast is to be firm in faith or devotion to duty. Steadfastness implies permanence, steadiness and/or immovability.

Your writing activities this week are based on the five synonyms of "steadfast" and/or "steadfastness."

<u>Monday</u>: *Firmness*. Do you know someone who has this trait? Who is this person in your life? How is she firm? Write about her for ten minutes.

<u>Tuesday</u>: *Loyal*. Animals can be loyal friends. Craft a short story about loyalty. Make your protagonist (your hero) an animal.

<u>Wednesday</u>: *Constant*. Friends come and go but there is that one friend who is always there. Who is this constant friend? Write about this friend for ten minutes.

<u>Thursday</u>: *Immovable*. Maybe you have heard of the phrase, "Immovable object meets irresistible force." Using this phrase as your prompt, what could be the immovable object and the irresistible force? Write about it for ten minutes.

<u>Friday</u>: *Permanence*. In your own words, define permanence. Then for ten to fifteen minutes, expound on your definition.

Millie is my best friend. She and I have known each other since we were six years old. We have been through it all. She is one of those rare friends you can call at 3 AM and it's no problem. We've nursed each other through bad breakups, deaths and between the two of us, the births of five children. We already know all of each other's secrets and stories, yet we can talk daily on the phone for hours and never run out of things to say. She is closer to me than a sister, and I love her very much.

# Week Twenty-One: Sobriety

Sobriety is a state of being moderate in temper or conduct; of forbearance; of self-denial; of calmness, sedateness and steadiness.

Below is a list of words that are synonymous and opposite in meaning to "sobriety" or "sober." They are your writing prompts this week. Use the three writing techniques you have learned – freewriting, brainstorming and word stringing – for your creative pieces.

Monday:
- unimpassioned
- subdued
- unexcited

Tuesday:
- frantic
- passionate
- unreasonable

Wednesday:
- extreme
- abstinence
- graveness

Thursday:
- balance
- intoxicating
- gluttony

<u>Friday</u>:
- agitation
- self-denial
- sedate

# Week Twenty-Two: Absurdities

Do you know that in Colombia, an old military policy was to airdrop photos of women to Marxist rebel camps to entice the rebels to defect?

In China, there were plans to execute five monkeys by firing squad after they terrorized park visitors. However, many protested so the monkeys were exiled to a faraway island instead.

In October 2002 in Missouri, a man was killed by a freight train after he stepped right in front of it. He had been talking on his cell phone and kept on walking.

Pretty weird or absurd, huh? They all happened, though. There are still many more weird and absurd things happening around the world as you read this.

This week, you will build stories from weird or absurd news. Here is a list of absurd or weird news. How did these things happen? Why did they happen? What happened next? You fill in the details.

<u>Monday</u>: A female train driver files a $25,000 lawsuit against her employer after she bruises a fingernail while adjusting the driver seat.

<u>Tuesday</u>: A man robs a convenience store and as a mask, he slathers shaving cream on his face.

<u>Wednesday</u>: In an attempt to get a date, a man in Turin, Italy arranges at least 500 bump-and-stop car accidents with young female drivers.

<u>Thursday</u>: A tele-marketer becomes a hero after calling a man and trying to sell him more minutes for his out-of-minutes wireless phone. The man was trapped in a blizzard in the Andes Mountains when she called.

<u>Friday</u>: Police captures a man driving a stolen truck. He denies he was trying to escape and instead says he could not stop because there was a bomb in the truck and it would explode if his speed dropped below 55 mph.

If you need any more weird or absurd news ideas to start off your stories, you will find plenty of them here: http://www.newsoftheweird.com/

Jan felt great that Monday morning. The weekend was good but it felt even better going back to work. She had a $100 manicure and she was looking forward to the comments from her co-workers and riders.

She glanced at her fingernails. They were bright red, highlighted with gold sparkles. She settled into her seat and prepared to leave the garage. Darn, she thought. Joe must have been driving this weekend. The seat was all out of adjustment. Her feet could barely reach the pedals. She carefully adjusted the seat when she felt a sharp pain in her finger. When she looked at it she saw the nail had been torn off and the finger was bruised. She could get blood poisoning. She hurriedly wrapped the finger and drover herself to the hospital.

She sat for hours in the emergency room waiting to get treatment. The more she thought about it, the angrier she became. She had warned the company the seats didn't adjust right. It was their fault she hurt her finger. The doctor was a comedian. She was going to live and probably not lose her finger, he told her sarcastically. Jan felt her good feeling finally leave her. It was almost 4:00 PM and she had missed work that day.

When she returned to the terminal, they told her she would be docked a day's pay. That was the last straw. A great day turned miserable when they were too cheap to fix a simple switch. Not only would she sue them for her pay but she would also sue them for pain and suffering. That would teach them a lesson - a $25,000 lesson.

Copyright © 2003 by Sarah E. Miller

## Week Twenty-Three: Disguises

A disguise is an attempt to conceal something – an appearance or a sound. It can be a simple disguise or an elaborate one.

One of the things I often do is disguise who I am on the phone each time I get a prank call (e.g., from a male looking for a phone friend at 2 a.m.). As soon as I hear, "Can you be my phone pal?" something clicks and I put on the worst accent I could muster and reply, "Yes! My name is Juana and I'm a maid. What's your name?" I would be talking to a dial tone by the time I finished my enthusiastic introduction.

A pen name is a disguise many writers use. Some writers use a pen name when they write in another genre. One of the reasons they do this is that they are quite established or known in another genre (e.g., children's books) and using a pen name will help 'protect' them when they write in another (e.g. romance or adult novels).

Shakespeare used a lot of disguises in his plays – women dressing up as men, two people swapping identities, etc.

This week, you will write about disguises. Devote five to twenty minutes on each prompt.

Monday: You can be anyone, except yourself, at a friend's party. Who would you be? What personality would you have? Is it going to be the opposite of who you really are? Will this reflect on your manner of clothing, the way you talk with people, and how you stand up, hold your drink or laugh?

Tuesday and Wednesday: Do you sometimes wish you did not stand out? Or was there a time you wished people did not notice you easily? Recall one of those times. What made you stand out? Why did you not want to stand out?

Thursday: Create a word string starting for the word, "DISGUISE". Come up with ten to fifteen words and use all of them in a story, essay or poem.

Friday: Think of a pen name for yourself. Even if you do not plan to use a pen name, go ahead and think of one for today's writing activity. Give yourself new first and last names. For ten to fifteen minutes, assume your new name. What kind of writer are you with this pen name? What will you write about? Do not worry if you are not really going to write in an unfamiliar genre. Just let your new name have its own 'writer personality.'

# Week Twenty-Four: Frames

When something happens to us, we tend to stare straight ahead and only see the sight unfolding before us. However, it is important to see how a moment fits in with the rest of our scene – how it fits in the bigger picture.

If you are dining in a restaurant and you are asked to write about the food, do you only describe how the food looked and how it tasted? Or do you notice other details – perhaps how the colors of the wall panels blended and enhanced the atmosphere? Or the crispness of the waiter's lapel?

As a writer, take, feel and sense everything so that when it is time for you to sit down and write, you will be able to take not just a flat close up of something, but a panorama of the place where your something fits in.

This week, go through your old photo albums. Find at least five photos (one for each day this week) with you or someone in your family in them. It can be a class picture, a birthday party, graduation day... anything.

Choose one photo for today's writing activity. Reserve the other four for the rest of the week. Look at the photo for three to five minutes. Recall as many details as you can about the event that was captured in the photo.

For five minutes, write about the surroundings or the place where that photo was taken. Do not focus on you or the people in the photo yet. Where was the photo taken? What was that place? How can someone get there? This is your panorama.

When the five minutes are up, stop and look at the photo again for another three minutes.

Then for another five minutes, write about you or the people in the photo. What were you (or they) doing? Why were you (or they) there? Why were you (or they) wearing those clothes; smiling; frowning; or wearing that expression? This is your close up.

The photo was taken at Ooty Botanical Garden in April 1997. Ooty Botanical Garden is familiar to people in India, particularly to those who love the hill stations, have been to Ooty or perhaps are film lovers! Many films in various Indian languages have been shot in this garden. The flower lovers can never escape this wonderful place. The grass is marvelous.

Ooty Botanical Garden is located in Ooty, which is situated in the Tamil Nadu State of India. There are two ways to get to Ooty - by road or by rail.

The background shows a road, the path to the upper side of the garden. Public vehicles are not permitted; only the authorities can use it.

We were on a holiday at Ooty for five days and we went to one of our favorite holiday spots in the hill station - the garden.

We (my parents, younger brother and I) were wondering who could take our family photo. People were sitting a little far. It was at that point that a girl who looked about four years old came by our way. We asked her name and which class she was studying. We teasingly asked her if she could take our photo. She replied positively. We weren't too sure if she could take it, yet my father told her how to hold the camera, focus and click the button. When asked, she said she could see us clearly. And there went the button, "Click!"

We couldn't control our smiles. We were thinking if the girl could really shoot a photo. I stood while my parents and brother sat in front of me. I had pulled my hair to two sides; it wasn't too long and my smile showed how I felt at that moment. So did it show in my parents' and brothers' faces. My brother, Roop, was wearing a hat, and he was holding his coat in his hand. I had the camera bag slung on my shoulders, and my mother was holding her handbag tightly. My father was his usual self, his posture comfortable.

The photo came out well, maybe even better than a photo an older person could have taken for us!

## Week Twenty-Five: Secrets

This week's Weekly Write activity is short and sweet. It involves only one question: "What are your secrets?"

Make a list of all your secrets, then write about one secret for each day of this week.

Fictionalize your secrets if you want. Use them as plots for short stories. Write your stories in the third person. Change names of people involved (you or somebody else).

Begin each day with ten to fifteen minutes of freewriting about a secret and then go on from there.

# Week Twenty-Six: Rings

Rings and circles have long symbolized infinity, an unending loop, a perpetual cycle.

<u>Monday</u>: List the names of all your friends, past and present. Begin with friends you had when you were a child, then when you were a teen, and so on.

Write a short description – one to two sentences – for each friend. When you are done, leave your list. You are done for the day.

<u>Tuesday</u>: Take a blank page and draw a small circle in the center. Inside the circle, write your name. Next, draw a circle around your circle. In that circle, write the names of friends who used to be or who still are the closest to you. Repeat this until you have used up all the names on your list. Finish it up by labeling each circle. Write a word or a phrase to describe the degree of friendship you used to share or still share with these people. The closer their ring is to you, the closer the degree of friendship you shared or are sharing with them.

<u>Wednesday, Thursday and Friday</u>: For each of the remaining days this week, choose one friend in your friendship ring and write about that friend. Write for ten to fifteen minutes.

# Week Twenty-Seven: Choices

Below is a list of choices for you. Simply choose one and then write about it for ten to fifteen minutes, or create word strings and go on from there.

Monday:
- a long bath or a hot shower?
- public transport or car?
- antique or modern?

Tuesday:
- elevator or stairs?
- candles or lights?
- theater or carnival?

Wednesday:
- letter or e-mail
- leisurely walk or frantic run?
- wine or soda?

Thursday:
- dine in or to-go?
- jeans and shirt or suit and tie?
- meat and potatoes or eggs and salad?

Friday:
- small groups or parties?

- suite or deluxe room?

- team sports or solo sports?

- first class or economy?

I came in from working in the yard. All I wanted was a hot shower and some down time. Unfortunately there was no hot water; seems daughter had decided to do her laundry. That's fine by me, but not when I want a shower!

I like to ride in a car; I do not like to drive. I prefer to be the passenger; I'll even navigate, just don't make me drive. I can drive; I just don't feel comfortable behind the wheel. Why do we use that phrase, "behind the wheel"? Where did it come from and when did it enter the language? Cars are odd creatures. Some of them have the most uncomfortable seats yet people buy them. Some come with all the conveniences of home and yet others are somewhere in between... Like I said, I like riding in a car. It is soothing to me, but driving is nerve wracking.

It was one of the most pleasant evenings I ever spent with some friends at a local restaurant. We ordered our meal and savored the appetizers, drank wine, had our salads and then our main dish came. The atmosphere was conducive to private chatter and we talked about everything under the sun and the moon. It wasn't a silent meal nor a hurried one. The food was delicious and the company was wonderful.

# Week Twenty-Eight: Tales

Stories are powerful. They let our imaginations run free. This is the reason books and films like The Lord of the Rings and Harry Potter are popular. This is the reason many films and books are based on myths and fairy tales (e.g., Ever After, First Knight, Dragon Heart).

This week, you will revisit fairy tales, and write your own.

<u>Monday, Tuesday and Wednesday</u>: Pick a fairy tale. During the next three days, re-write the fairy tale from the point of view of one of its characters. Notice how the story 'shifts' or 'changes' when different characters tell their version of the tale.

Variation: Work on three fairy tales, one fairy tale a day and several points of view per day.

<u>Thursday</u>: Change the setting of your chosen fairy tale. Put the characters in today's setting. Do not discard the magic or the other fairy tale aspects, only discard the setting.

<u>Friday</u>: In fairy tales, protagonists are always faced with challenges. In the end, they are able to overcome those challenges and well... live happily ever after.

Today, think of yourself as the protagonist in a fairy tale... your fairy tale. What challenges are you facing right now? Financial challenges? Relationship challenges? Career challenges? Choose one and write your fairy tale. Add any fairy tale ingredients: dragons, wicked witch or stepmother, frog, magic wands, magic beans, poisoned apples. And do not forget to give your fairy tale a happy ending.

# Week Twenty-Nine: Voices

Author Shirley Kawa-Jump wrote: "All authors, whether they realize it or not, have a common theme running through their work, whether it is the strength of love, the theme of redemption, the saving power of truth, etc. Your theme is part of your fingerprint on your work and is part of what makes your writing sound uniquely yours."

For your writing activities this week, below is a list of themes for you to write about, one theme per day.

For each theme, brainstorm and list three to five images or scenes that embody that theme. Then do three five-minute freewriting sessions for each theme so that at the end of the week, you will have fifteen rough drafts to develop further and use to hone your writing voice.

<u>Monday</u>: Rediscovering love

<u>Tuesday</u>: Forgiveness

<u>Wednesday</u>: Freedom

<u>Thursday</u>: Finding strength in faith

<u>Friday</u>: Expansiveness of the universe

Resources to help you find your writing voice:

- Finding Your Voice
  http://www.write4kids.com/feature3.html

- Ten Steps to Finding Your Writing Voice
  http://hollylisle.com/fm/Articles/wc1-6.html

- Knowing and Finding Your Voice
  http://writingcorner.com/nonfiction/stronger-writing/skj-voice.htm

- Finding Your Voice
  http://www.efuse.com/Design/wa-voice.html

# Week Thirty: Images

When you are being creative, you are using your right brain. Writing is a creative process so when you write, your right brain thinks in images then it quickly transforms those images into words. This transformation is almost instantaneous and done in an unconscious level.

This week, you will work on images and then transform these images into words.

Below are images for you to work on – one image per day. Either freewrite, brainstorm or do a word string on each image for five to ten minutes. Evoke the five senses – sight, touch, smell, sound and taste.

Monday: Your dream vacation

Tuesday: Your first teacher

Wednesday: Your first/last/best boss

Thursday: A memorable holiday

Friday: A memorable gift

My love for snow and mountains could have never been satisfied had I not set foot on Shimla, one of most beautiful locales in the country. Anyone with love for the mountains will die to be at Shimla.

It is so chilly and charming. True...God exists. Shimla does make me feel this. The clock on the church at the mall area looks exactly like I had pictured in my painting. And the snow fallen all over the place... on the ground, over the trees, behind the church. No wonder people kept asking if I had been to this beautiful locale earlier! It was as if the place was my creation!

The scent of the eucalyptus trees around clears my throat and makes me breathe well. I could get rid of the damn attack of cold.

The hill is so silent, except for the occasional sounds of "huh" and "phew" from the visitors. Motors are occasionally seen. How much I love this tiny hill station. I could spend the rest of my life here.

My first touch of snow. Something I longed for all my life after hearing descriptions of my father's life in the northern parts of India during the 60s and 70s. Snow. It is softer than I had thought it would be. My gloves. Oh! I wish I could remove the gloves so I could dig into the snow with my hand, sit on the snow or perhaps sleep there for a night. Life would be so sweet in the snow-clad mountain.

Snow has started to fall again. I can feel the slow, tender touch of the mountains.

Snow, You have made it,
Made my day,
And a life
To move ahead
Encounter the ruthless
City life,
for your memories,
Can make me move on

As I continue with my walk, I look around the enchanting beauty of the hills. I wrapped them in my memory and heart.

Shoot! It was all a dream; a dream I wish would happen for real… to feel the power of snow, the tender touch, the aroma of the plants around. One day, I'll be there… on my dream vacation.

# Week Thirty-One: Eloquence

Merriam-Webster Dictionary defines eloquence as "the quality of forceful or persuasive expressiveness."

As a writer, words are your means of persuasion. Whether you write fiction or nonfiction, your two main purposes are to catch and hold your readers' attention and make them interested in what you are writing about.

Here are tips for writing persuasively:

1. Define or introduce the problem/issue that forms your subject.

2. Analyze the problem/issue by giving specific examples.

3. Mention opposing points of view and analyze them to show their strengths and weaknesses.

4. Avoid oversimplifying the problem/issue.

5. Give solutions to the problem/issue.

6. End your piece with your most convincing material either by giving a brief restatement of solutions, analogy or a quote from an authority.

7. Support your argument throughout the main body of your piece.

8. Strengthen your arguments by stating your qualifications.

9. Appeal to your readers' interests and sympathies.

Monday and Tuesday: Choose a recent editorial from a local newspaper and write a 500-word piece that explains why you agree or disagree with it.

Wednesday: What change do you think is most needed at the school or office you are attending?

Thursday: What annoying habit does a friend or family member have that you think can be corrected? Write a letter to him that persuades him to break the habit.

Friday: What area do you need to improve on? Persuade yourself to improve by writing yourself a letter.

# Week Thirty-Two: Customs

Dating is rare in Afghanistan because parents arrange marriages and schools are separate for boys and girls.

In Indonesia, it is considered extremely rude to point to a person with the forefinger. When pointing, the Indonesian uses his thumb.

In Thailand, it is a grave insult to walk into a person's house with shoes on. Shoes are discarded at the front door.

The above are only some of the customs and traditions around the world. A country's customs and traditions may be commonplace to those living in that country and inhabitants of surrounding countries but may be strange and peculiar to others.

This week, you will do two things: write about existing customs and traditions, and create your own customs and traditions.

<u>Monday and Tuesday</u>: Generate a list of customs and traditions for the following areas:

- bathing
- wedding
- dating
- funerals
- birthdays
- kissing
- fashion/dress
- farewells

- worshipping
- eating/meals
- transportation

Use the Internet to come up with your list of customs and traditions. Make your list as diverse as possible.

Next, choose one (or more if you prefer) from your generated list and write about it.

<u>Wednesday, Thursday and Friday</u>: Invent your own customs and traditions for the areas I have enumerated above. Then for each of the remaining days, pick a custom or tradition and write about it – explain what it is or use it in a story or poem.

Greeting People: People are welcomed by saying "Namaste", folding two hands, and bringing the palms together.

Cuisine: Dishes the combine coconut and seafood are more popular in the region. Traditionally, people used to consume kanji (rice soup). Today, there are a wide variety of dishes in South Indian restaurants, which are popular the world over. Tea is an all time favourite of Keralites. Coffee is the second choice. Black tea (tea without milk) is popular. Malayalis also take a lot of spices. Food is eaten with hand. Banana leaves, though used to act as vessel for eating food in the olden days, are now used only for giving feasts during marriage ceremonies or festive occasions.

Dress: The traditional dress of Kerala women is Neryathu (white mundu - dhoti with a cloth draped over the shoulder along with a blouse). Today, most of the women wear saris (six meters of cloth) or Churidars. Among the younger generation, Churidars and other modern dresses top the list. Muslim women of some communities still stick on to the tradition and wear full purdah. Most of the men, especially those who live in the cities, wear the Western-style dress, shirts and full trousers. Occasionally, men are seen wearing Kasavu Mundu, the traditional attire of Malayali men. Informally, men wear coloured Mundu known as Lungi.

All said, the younger generation prefers Western outfits, and what was once considered as totally unacceptable, such as shorts and mini skirts, are now part of the clothing style of the upper class and high middle class families in Kerala.

It's remarkable to note that it is most often difficult to make out if a man is rich or poor because he makes it a point to dress neatly of whatever he possesses.

Dating: Dating was unknown in Kerala until very recently. The culture of the State doesn't accept dating, although times are changing and it's not uncommon to see youngsters dating.

Live-in relationships are debarred. Those who dare plunge into live-in relationships bring the wrath of society upon themselves.

Marriages: Wedding ceremonies depend on the religion and also on the sub-castes within each religion. Hindu marriages, except in cases of Brahmin communities and the like, have a short ceremony, which lasts for 5-15 minutes. Matching the horoscopes of the bride and groom is considered important in Hindu communities.

Most marriages are arranged. Parents find the groom for their daughter. If the girl and the boy like each other, marriage happens following customary norms. Dowry is a part of most marriages, irrespective of community. Earlier, dowry was a

117

customary act. Today, however, it is considered an evil because of the after effects, e.g., the girl and her family undergo trauma in most cases.

Family life: The older days saw joint families. When the cities emerged, families split up to form nuclear families. Children live with their parents at home until the girl marries or the boy leaves for a job far away. Girls, too, go to far away places for work but unlike in the West where teenagers live independently, this phenomenon doesn't exist in Kerala.

Language: People in Kerala talk in their native language, Malayalam. Some people in Kerala also speak Tamil, the native language of the neighbouring state, Tamil Nadu. English is known to most people. Occasionally, educated people would speak Hindi, the national language of India.

# Week Thirty-Three: Waves

This week, you will take your cue from pictures.

<u>Monday</u>: *The View from My Window*

Visit http://ewritersplace.com/images/001.jpg

It is morning. You open your window and this is the view that greets you. How do you feel? What thoughts run through your head as you behold the view in front of you? Write for ten minutes.

<u>Tuesday</u>: *My Far-Away Island*

Visit http://ewritersplace.com/images/002.jpg

This is your own island. You can see how far it is from the nearest islands. Describe your island. How long have you lived here? Why do you live here? Write for ten minutes.

<u>Wednesday</u>: *The Place I Used to Live*

Visit http://ewritersplace.com/images/003.jpg

You used to live on those islands. What made you leave? What kind of life did you lead when you lived there? Who were the people you left? What did you leave behind? Write for ten minutes.

<u>Thursday</u>: *The Calm in My Ocean*

Visit http://ewritersplace.com/images/004.jpg

Look at the photo for three minutes. What effect does it have on your emotions? Describe it. Write for ten minutes.

Friday: *The Mood of the Waves*

Visit http://ewritersplace.com/images/005.jpg

Look at the photo for three minutes. If you were to give a human attribute to the water/wave, what would it be? Write about it for ten minutes.

This is my island. I call it Writer's Dream. My uncle died about six years ago and left the island to me. At first I did nothing with it. I mean, what do you do with an island? One day, when I was sick and tired of the city and the whole day-to-day drudgery of life as a journalist, I decided I needed a vacation. I decided to check out my island. Uncle Mick used the island for vacations. As far as I know he hadn't been there for years, but someone had been. The staff. I had a staff! I immediately fell in love with my island and decided to quit my job at the paper and finally settle down to write my novel. I did just that. Then another and another. After the third bestseller, I named the island Writer's Dream because it was a dream come true. To have such a beautiful place to spark the creativity in me like nothing ever had...

# Week Thirty-Four: Portraits

There are two essential steps involved in this week's writing activities:

1. Write your name in big bold letters on top of a blank page.

2. Beginning with the first letter of your name, write down all the adjectives you can think of that start with it. When you cannot think of an adjective anymore, move on to the next letter and repeat the process.

<u>Monday and Tuesday</u>: Pick one adjective from your list of adjectives. Based on that adjective, list reasons or specific examples that illustrate you are that adjective. Then begin a factual or even fictional character sketch based on your examples.

<u>Wednesday, Thursday and Friday</u>: Do the two steps above for the names of your family members and friends. Create fictional characters based on their personalities, or write their stories, memoir-style, and compile them.

# Week Thirty-Five: Byways

A byway is a little traveled side road. Very rarely do people pass this road. Why? For many reasons... it may be because it is narrow, difficult to pass (steep, dangerous, winding) or 'too out of the way' from one's true destination. The list goes on.

Reflect on your life – what you have done, how far along you have come, the journeys you have taken – and think of the little byways you traveled on and the byways you did not take.

Your byways can be anything. They are symbols of your life journeys.

Byways can be the college course you did not take; the man or woman you did not marry; the friendships you did not keep; the career opportunities you passed up; the choices you did not make. You had your reasons for not choosing to travel on these byways.

And for the byways you did take, you, too, had a reason for traveling on them.

For your writing activities this week, make two lists: a list of byways you took and a list of byways you did not take.

Then for each day, choose one from each list and freewrite on them for five minutes.

# Week Thirty-Six: Preparations

<u>Monday and Wednesday</u>: How do you prepare for special occasions?

Think of an occasion – birthday, anniversary, graduation – and describe the things you and your family did to prepare for that occasion. Write for five minutes. When the five minutes are up, look over what you wrote. Choose a scene and then write more about it.

<u>Tuesday and Thursday</u>: How do you prepare for the arrival of a child, a parent, a relative or a friend?

Recall a time when you received news a person close to you was arriving or coming home. This person could be a child who has been away for summer camp, college or a long vacation; a parent you have not seen in years; a relative from out of state; or a dear friend. Then for five minutes, write about how you prepared for her homecoming.

<u>Friday</u>: Think of someone you most admire. This someone could be anyone – your favorite author, singer, politician, artist. Imagine receiving a letter of a phone call from this person. He tells you he will be stopping by your house for lunch two days from today. How would you prepare for his visit? What questions will you ask him? Write about it for five to ten minutes.

A few more suggestions:

- How do you prepare for a test?
- How do you prepare for a job interview?
- What preparations do you do before a long trip? short trip?

- How did you prepare for your wedding? (If you are single, how would you prepare for your wedding?)

The Job Interview (an excerpt)

Each interview you go to opens up a whole world of opportunities. "Be all you can be," are some famous words, which, within a different context, are so true. Every job interview gives you the opportunity to look into the deepest parts of yourself, your personality and your abilities. There is no place to doubt yourself, only to be the best and maybe even the boldest you can be.

Life is full of opportunities and with faith, hard work, determination and patience, the right door will open up. All you need then is the courage to take the doorknob into your hand and be all you can be. You know who you are and what you want. There is just one last problem. You do not know who your interviewer is and what is really expected from you.

So I forgot to mention that the road to success could still be a bit unpaved, even when you are fully empowered and capable. Anyway, remember that in this interview, what you say and how you carry yourself are crucial. But there is also fun! What do I mean? Everybody will hear what you say and see how you carry yourself, but nobody will know what you are thinking... those little cartoony captions floating over your head. Of course your counterpart, meaning the interviewer, also has his personal captions floating above his head. But bingo, there we go. Both of you already have something in common. You both don't know what to expect from each other and you both are concerned to make the right decision.

Let me tell you what happened at my last interview. First, I thought all my chances had flown out the window when the Human Resources person called and proposed a date and time for an interview. I just could not make it that day. What an impression. However, I got the famous second chance and the interview actually happened.

The night before, I read my way through the ad on the career link to get at least a mental picture what the job might be like. Distribution was one of the words in the description. Oh great, that sounded just like a big and dirty warehouse. No way would I fit into that kind of environment. Sweaty, smelly men who tell each other yesterday's heroic beer store stories. But wait, the job was supposed to be in a social environment, and I would be working part of the day in the billing department. That means probably one of those little cubicles where you have those idiotic headphones on that never work right. It could hardly be any worse than what I was already doing. What do I have to lose? I glanced over my résumé. That's me. I might not have the confidence at that point, but yes that is what I really know and am capable of.

The big day came. I told my boss I had a doctor's appointment. Of course, this was a lie—and I truly hated doing that—No, really, I did not mind lying to her because I could not stand being there. I rushed to that place up the street from my hopefully soon old job. I got there just in time, and had to do all those usual stuff, like filling out those never ending applications. It's one of those things I could never stand when I go to interviews. You give people your résumé, detailed enough, with your address and so on, and then they get back to you and let you manually fill out basically all the information again.

I didn't even know who was going to talk to me. Was it the HR person or a manager or my immediate supervisor to be?

"Good Afternoon, my name is-----" An approximately 35-year old man stood in front of me, reaching his hand out to greet me. What was his name? I forgot his name the second he said it. It meant I had to play this technical game of avoiding saying his name without letting him know I didn't know his name. Great. Not knowing the name of your interviewer is not a good way to start an interview...

# Week Thirty-Seven: Steps

Remember the last time you asked for directions? Did you ask for directions on how to reach a place or how to do something like cook a recipe or file for insurance? Were the directions clear? Were you able to get to where you were going or finish a task quickly and with the minimum amount of fuss? Or did something else happen?

This week's activity involves giving directions and all the necessary steps in undertaking a task.

The goal of this activity is to help you write more clearly, leaving no room for your reader to not understand you.

Before you tackle the prompts, think of someone. That someone can be a friend, a family member or a child. It can be someone who speaks a different language.

You will write for that someone. Assume she does not know anything so you have to provide complete details and directions as much as possible.

Monday:
- How to use a word processor.
- How to make a sandwich.

Tuesday:
- How to reach your house.
- How to start a campfire.

Wednesday:
- How to watch television.
- How to play baseball (or another sport).

Thursday:
- How to play solitaire.
- How to check out a book from the library.

Friday:
- How to buy things in the grocery.
- How to go shopping.

For a humorous example, see the online PowerPoint presentation of "How to Give a Cat a Pill" by going to http://www.phil-race.net/BitsnPieces/catPill.ppt.

# Week Thirty-Eight: Warnings

<u>Monday</u>: Think back to the time when you were a child. What were the things your mother or father warned you about? Make a list of these things, then pick one and freewrite for ten minutes.

<u>Tuesday</u>: Take a walk around town today. Are there any buildings or places that are off-limits? Do you see any "Do not trespass" signs hanging over fences, or "Condemned" signs on buildings? If there are no places or buildings like these where you live, make one up! Write about what the place or building might have looked like ten or fifteen years ago. What was the purpose of that building and who were the people that came in and out of it? Feel free to invent. Freewrite for ten minutes.

<u>Wednesday</u>: Traffic signs warn drivers about dangerous conditions. Warning signs are usually diamond-shaped and have a yellow background with black letters or symbols.
Visit this link:
http://www.ewritersplace.com/warningsigns.html. Pick one warning sign and use it as a story element.

<u>Thursday</u>: Cultures around the world have their own omens and superstitions. Make a list of omens and superstitions you know. Pick one omen or superstition and write about it. Do you believe in that omen? If yes, explain why you believe in it. If you do not, explain why you do not believe in it.

<u>Friday</u>: Create a superstitious society. Invent omens and superstitions and make these the driving forces behind actions of the people in your society.

For an example of a real superstitious society, go to this link: http://www.roman-empire.net/religion/superstitions.html.

# Week Thirty-Nine: Rebirths

For many of us, rebirth has different meanings. Below is a set of questions whose underlying theme is rebirth. Begin by freewriting for five to ten minutes.

<u>Monday</u>: When was a time you felt you were given a second chance?

<u>Tuesday</u>: If you could choose a name for yourself, what would it be?

<u>Wednesday</u>: You are given an opportunity to go back in time and be a part of history. What era would you travel back to and who would you be?

<u>Thursday</u>: You are given an opportunity to choose three talents or skills. What three talents or skills do you want to possess?

<u>Friday</u>: What is the meaning of rebirth for you?

# Week Forty: Expectations

To expect means to await, to anticipate or look forward to the coming or occurrence of something – it can be the arrival of a new child, a promotion, a career improvement or a homecoming.

What are your expectations?

Monday: What are some of the things you expect from your family? List ten to fifteen of these expectations, pick one and write about it for ten minutes.

Tuesday: What are some of the things you expect from your friends? List ten to fifteen of these expectations, pick one and write about it for ten minutes.

Wednesday: What are some of the things you expect from your co-workers? List ten to fifteen of these expectations, pick one and write about it for ten minutes.

Thursday: What are some of the things you expect from your town or city officials? List ten to fifteen of these expectations, pick one and write about it for ten minutes.

Friday: What are some of the things you expect from yourself? List ten to fifteen of these expectations, pick one and write about it for ten minutes.

A few more prompts:

• What things in your life do you expect to change for the better two months from now? six months from now? a year from now? five years from now?

- What are your hopes for your family?
- What are your hopes for yourself?
- What are your hopes for your community?
- What are your hopes for your career?

# Week Forty-One: Possibilities

Writers are a powerful lot. We control time. We dictate actions. We control destinies.

We can make two completely opposite people fall in love with each other. We can create family feuds that last for centuries. We can make our heroine travel back in time to rescue her soul mate. We can give the most villainous person the punishment she deserves. We can take our characters to the most exotic places and give them their own adventures.

Simply put, we can create our own possibilities. In our world, nothing is impossible.

This week, create your own possibilities using the given prompts below. There are four givens: theme, setting, character and key object. Randomly pick one from each and use these to start a different story every day.

For example: A doctor is your main character. Your story happens in a lab and a shoe plays a big part in your story. Your story is about irony.

Theme: deception, irony, love lost, infidelity
Setting: space colony, gym, park, lab
Character: chemist, divorced woman, doctor, teacher
Key object: yellow bag, pen, knife, shoe

# Week Forty-Two: Proverbs

"Proverbs...tell much about a people's traditional ways of experiencing reality, about the proper or expected ways of doing things, about values and warnings, and rules and wisdom the elders want to impress on the minds of their young. The punch line character of proverbs—the shorter the better—makes it easy to commit them to memory for ready recall when the occasion calls for serious or humorous comment or admonition."

(Source: http://www.serve.com/shea/germusa/prov1.htm)

This week, your writing will take off from proverbs. Use the given 'real' proverbs and 'mixed' proverbs below to start off your stories.

'Real' Proverbs:

1. An old broom knows the corners of the house.
2. Anything tastes good when you are hungry.
3. The morning hour has gold in its mouth.
4. People who live in glass houses shouldn't throw stones.
5. The belly has no conscience.

'Mixed' Proverbs:

1. Necessity strikes in the same place.
2. Lightning brings May flowers.
3. The proof of the pudding teaches success.
4. A rolling stone calls the kettle black.
5. Curiosity is blind.

# Week Forty-Three: Musings

Musing (or meditating) is an act of thinking reflectively, or simply contemplating.

This week's activity is simple enough – you will reflect about things, issues and people. You will not be skimming the surface; you will be going deep. Your musings may just be for your eyes only or you can develop them further.

Whatever path your musings or reflections take you, forget about your fears, trepidation, worries, doubts. Simply write; simply explore; simply let yourself go.

Monday: Make a list of fifty questions you have always wanted to know the answer to. This can range from "Where did I put my pair of earrings?" to "Why are there days I feel like I'm helpless?" When you are done with your list, stop. Keep your list in a safe place.

Tuesday, Wednesday, Thursday and Friday: Take out your list, pick one question and reflect on it. Write down everything you can think of that could relate to your question -- possible solutions, reasons and thoughts. Write for five to ten minutes.

List excerpt:

1. Why am I short? I don't feel short. I don't act short. I max out about 5'10". I may not really be that tall, but I think that's what my driver's license says. Anyway, I don't feel short. In fact, in my house, I'm tall. In fact, in my extended family, I'm tall (my brother-in-law, and one of my sisters, may be taller as well as my uncle, the spy). Being short is not really a handicap. I never expected to play in the NBA (believe it or

not, when I was MUCH younger, I could touch the rim) or in the NFL. When I was young and a tennis stud, even tennis players weren't tall. I'm taller than Eddie Dibbs and Harold Solomon as well as Guillermo Vilas who were all ranked in the Top 10 in the 1970s. I don't have problems buying pants that fit. I don't have to worry whether I'll fit in the bed. Heck, I can sleep on most full size sofas. I don't duck to go through doors, even on submarines. I can fit in the backseat of most cars, even though I look pretty funny extricating myself from the third seat of our van. I don't scare small children. So, I don't feel short, I just feel altitudinally adequate.

2. Who picks up the penny I stepped over? What do they do with it?

3. Why is it so easy to be friends with married women? Am I that "safe"? That's depressing. Hey, I'm not Jimmy Carter. I'm not about to make a public pronunciation of my lust for other women. Oh. No, I'm smarter than that. But let's face it; you want to feel dangerous once in a while. You'd like some guy to be a little jealous when you make his wife/girlfriend laugh. But no, they always say, "That's just Greg, the short (see #1), fat, SAFE guy. I don't have to worry about him." And truth be told, he doesn't. I love my wife, and my kids, and there's nothing out there better than what I have. Plus, why would I look for new sources of humiliation? I can get that at home.

4. What was I thinking?

5. Am I an overachiever with minimal skills, or am I an underachiever who has wasted wonderful skills?

6. Where do all the lost socks go?

7. The jar states "Do Not Use If Seal Is Broken." How do I get to the food?

8. I'm much smarter than Mike Tyson. Why did he make $300 million dollars, and not me? And why did he squander it? Who's smarter after all?

9. I'm a republican. Why do I like Tipper Gore so much? Okay since we're talking about older women, let's go ahead and get to Tipper Gore. Al, you're a wooden dolt, but you did at least three cool things in your life: You roomed with Tommy Lee Jones in college; you invented the Internet; you married Tipper. C'mon, let's face it; Tipper's a 55 year-old former Second Lady babe. Hey, she used to play drums in a rock band. Her kids are relatively cool. She and Al (according to *Rolling Stone)* even went to see Fountains of Wayne (*Stacey's Mom*) in D.C. Having Tipper as First Lady would have almost made up for Al. Well, almost.

10. My wife occasionally has music faxed to her. What would Beethoven and Mozart have done if they could have faxed music back and forth?

11. When did "Not Me" move into my house, and who invited them?

12. We are totally incapable of keeping houseplants and fish alive. How did the fiddler crab live for so long?

13. Are you really delegating authority, or just making someone else do your work?

14. Why do brides put such horrible pictures in the paper? I have an admission to make. Every Sunday, after perusing the Sports section and drooling over stuff I can't afford in the

Best Buy circular, I go to the Life & Arts section. Yes, I want to read the book reviews, and of course I've got to read Dave Barry, possibly the funniest writer alive today. But, after that, do I set the paper aside? Absolutely not! I go to the wedding section, which has its own intrinsic humor. Ladies, why do you do this to yourself? You are celebrating what should be the grandest day of your life, and you commemorate it with pictures that make you look like Elsa Lanchester in The Bride of Frankenstein. It's a hoot. You see these brides in their ridiculously expensive and ridiculous looking dresses, always trying to show an excessive amount of cleavage. Some hack photographer has posed them in a simply unnatural pose, often using some prop. (I once saw a bride holding a beautiful crystal-cut glass of ICED TEA. How stupid can that be?)

15. Who said all babies are beautiful? What were they thinking?

16. Yes, no, n/a. Why not other?

17. If I can download any song for 99 cents, why does the store want to charge me $14.99 for 12 of them on a CD, 6 of which I don't want anyway? I have usually avoided the music downloading discussions here, because most of you don't care, but I've got to say something. What are the record companies thinking? They are suing their customers because their customers are tired of playing by the industry's rules. The music buying public wants to continue to acquire music, but we want to do it on our own terms. We don't want to have to pay ever-increasing prices for product, which frankly, is crap. Please stop making full length CDs and charging $17 dollars for them. Let people buy music by the song. Stop trying to sell me reissues and greatest hits packages of 30-year-old music for 5 times what I paid for it on vinyl in 1973. Yeah, we'll download a few free songs from

Kazaa, but we're likely to enjoy that music and BUY some of it. RIAA, figure this out, and let me enjoy my music.

18. Who said *Stairway to Heaven* is the best song of all time? Who decided *that?*

19. Did Pete Townshend really write *Tommy* so Schering could sell Clarinex?

20. If someone's "dumber than rock salt", how dumb are they?

21. Why does "Reality TV" seem so unreal to me?

22. Do dogs eat broccoli? Why? Doesn't it give them gas, like it does me?

23. Would people go hunting if the deer had guns too?

24. Would anybody even bother to record "Alice's Restaurant" today? Would a record label let them?

25. Why is bottled water more expensive than soft drinks?

# Week Forty-Four: Pressures

When I was in grade school, I felt pressured to memorize prayers and songs. I went to a Catholic school run by nuns. I was also pressured to do extremely well in class and keep myself in the honors list year after year.

When it was time to enter high school, I opted to go to a secular school. There were no religion subjects, but the pressure to fit in took the place of the pressures I had in the old school.

In college, pressures came from all sides: the pressure to be identified with an organization or a sorority, the pressure to not fail course, the pressure to maintain my status as a 'regular' student in order to always get a full load of classes each semester and not be left behind, the pressure to finish my thesis and graduate on time.

And then there were (and still are) family pressures and job pressures. And there is the kind of pressures I knowingly and unknowingly give myself.

Pressures, when they take on an unbearable intensity, can wear us out, leave us depressed, and even render us demotivated. There are times we might buckle under pressure and stop functioning altogether, but there are times we rise up and do well.

This week, you will explore your past and current pressures. You will examine what bearing your past pressures have on your present life and what you can do about your current pressures.

Monday: Today make two lists: your Past Pressures list and your Current Pressures list. Come up with at least twenty pressures for each list. Your pressures can range from the simple to the more complex pressures. Devote at around ten minutes for each list.

Tuesday and Wednesday: Pick one pressure from your Past Pressures list and describe the pressure in detail. How did you feel? What did you do? Did that particular pressure have a significant effect on the life you are living now or on the way you think/view things?

Thursday and Friday: Pick one pressure from your Current Pressures list and describe the pressure in detail. How does the current pressure make you feel? What could be the cause of this current pressure? What are you going to do about it? Have you encountered this same pressure before? If you have, how did you deal with it?

Keep the list you have made. When you find other writing time, work on them some more.

# Week Forty-Five: Self-Image

People oftentimes see themselves based on how others see them. How do you see yourself? How do you perceive yourself?

This week, you will write about how you see yourself. You will write about your self-image. And you will take an active part in eliminating the negative perceptions you have unconsciously formed about yourself.

Monday: Make a list of forty affirmations about yourself. Affirmations are positive statements. Begin each affirmation with "I am..." If you find yourself thinking negative statements, quickly transform those statements into positive statements. For example, if you are thinking of writing, "I am disorganized," change that into "I am a creative." When you are done with your list, read it over and then keep it somewhere safe.

Tuesday and Wednesday: Take out your list of forty affirmations. Pick one affirmation and write about it. For example, one of your affirmations is "I am a creative." What makes you one? What are the creative things you engage in? How do you feel whenever you set out to do something creative? Do you feel fulfilled? Do you feel proud? Do you feel energized?

Thursday: Imagine receiving a letter from an editor or a publisher. It is an acceptance letter. Describe yourself as the scene unfolds. Is it an acceptance for an article? Is it an acceptance for your novel? Do not restrain yourself and your emotions. Do this for ten to fifteen minutes.

Friday: Close your eyes and think of the kind of writer you aspire to become – your ideal writer. Write about it for ten minutes. Write as if you are your ideal writer. Write in the present tense.

# Week Forty-Six: Legacy

This week, you will look at the gifts you have received from the past, and gifts you want to leave for the future. These are your legacies. They are the blessings you have received and wish to pass on, be they big or small, significant or not too significant.

<u>Monday, Tuesday and Wednesday</u>: Make a list of things you have received from your family and relatives. They can be anything from your grandmother's comb to the watch your father gave you on your twenty-first birthday. Do this for five minutes. Next, choose one from your list and write about it for ten minutes. Who gave it to you? When was it given to you? Do you still have it with you today? What is the most vivid memory attached to it? Write fast and do not censor yourself.

<u>Thursday</u>: You are the ancestor this time. Today, make a Tangible Legacies list. List ten to fifteen tangible gifts you would like to leave to your descendants. Devote five minutes for this. When you are done, choose one and write about it for ten minutes. What is the significance of your chosen tangible legacy to future generations? Write from the point of view of your great-grandson or great-granddaughter who has just discovered this tangible legacy.

<u>Friday</u>: Again, you are the ancestor. Today, make an Intangible Legacies list. List ten to fifteen intangible gifts you would like to leave to your descendants. Devote five minutes for this. When you are done, choose one and write about it for ten minutes. Write from the point of view of your great-nephew or great-niece who has just discovered or found out about this intangible legacy.

I was 21 years old, and spending Christmas with my family at my parents' home. As we finished opening gifts, my father stood slowly and said he'd be right back. I wasn't paying too much attention to what he was doing, but I could see him out of the corner of my eye, bent over like a worn tin soldier, rummaging through a drawer in his bedroom.

He came back and handed me a small gift. "Be careful," he warned me, "this one is special." I gave him a questioning look and took the clumsily wrapped gift from his strong hand. It was wrapped in red paper, Scotch-taped to the point where it was almost impossible to open. He watched my every move with his steel blue eyes, never blinking, and I pondered what in the world it could be. The wrapping paper came off in a coil, around and around and around the gift it went, shrinking the gift to about half its wrapped size.

I started laughing. "I can tell you wrapped this, Dad."

He smiled, something rare and beautiful. I smiled back and turned my gaze to the gift that had fallen into my shaking hand.

I dropped the wrapping paper as tears filled my eyes, and I looked up at my father.

Inside the wrapping paper was a small toy, very old and worn as if it had been continually played with in its life span. The toy was Snoopy, my favorite cartoon character with that sly smile on his face, wearing a blue cap and sitting in a blue and white mail truck. My hands were shaking and I was trying so hard not to cry, because I felt I would look ridiculous crying over a toy. I put the truck on the rug and pushed it across the floor to my father, who knelt down and picked it up.

"So?" he asked, with a shrug. "What do you think?"

"You saved it," I said quietly, disbelievingly. Memories of my being a little girl flooded my soul like warm water, and the tears slid down my cheek. I was unable to stop them.

"All these years," he concurred, tears filling his eyes too. "I thought you'd want it, but I didn't know when to give it to you."

"Thank you," I whispered. I seemed to have lost my voice.

The Snoopy truck had been my toy from when I was only six years old. Though it had already been mine once, I couldn't think of a gift I would have much rather received at that time in my life. That toy showed me as clear as day the love my father had for me that would continue throughout the rest of his life.

My father passed away in October of 2000, and I never doubt the love he had for me-especially when I look at the toy, which holds a special place on my bedroom dresser.

# Week Forty-Seven: Keepsakes

This week's writing theme is an extension of last week's Legacy theme.

Bring out the first list you made last Monday. It is the list of things you have received from your family and relatives. Pick five keepsakes from your list. You will work on one keepsake per day this week.

<u>Monday, Tuesday, Wednesday, Thursday and Friday</u>: For each keepsake, think of a person, a relative, a family member, even future grandsons and granddaughters, you would like to give the keepsake. Write him or her a letter about the keepsake and why you chose him or her to own it. Tell him or her how much you value the keepsake. Write for ten to fifteen minutes.

At the end of this activity, you can put the letters and the keepsakes in envelopes and seal them. Keep them in a safe place. When you think the time is right, give them to the people you chose to give them to.

# Week Forty-Eight: Firsts

First date. First kiss. First love.

Remember the time you first fell in love, or you thought you were in love and everyone told you it was only "puppy love"?

Remember when the handsomest boy in class asked you to be his date for junior prom? Or the prettiest girl in school agreed to go out with you?

Do you remember the first date? How about the first kiss? Can you still smell the scent of the first bouquet of flowers he sent you? Remember how you felt the first time she sat in the passenger seat and you drove her around town?

The memory of first love is perhaps one of the few memories we never really forget.

<u>Monday</u>: For ten to fifteen minutes, freewrite using the prompt, "When I was (your age here), there was this boy/girl. And his/her name was..."

<u>Tuesday</u>: Write a thank-you letter to your spouse or partner. Write about the good things your spouse or partner has done for you since you met him or her. How has he or she helped you grow as a person? Write from your heart and leave no room for embarrassment. Your partner deserves to know what you think of his or her presence in your life. This is your gratitude letter.

If you are not married or in a relationship, then write a thank-you letter to someone who has been present in your life for a long time – a parent, a sibling, a relative, a dear friend.

<u>Wednesday</u>: What is the perfect love letter for you? What does it contain? What does it express? Imagine you are writing the love letter to yourself. Write for ten to fifteen minutes.

<u>Thursday</u>: Recall past relationships. If you were to give each of them a theme song, what would it be? Write about this for fifteen to twenty minutes.

<u>Friday</u>: Make a list of twenty to thirty things you associate 'Love' with. It can be a thing, a memory, a person, something intangible. Then choose one from your list and write about it for ten minutes.

## Week Forty-Nine: Growth

Growth is an integral part of life. It is a given. We grow – physically, mentally, emotionally, socially and spiritually. Growth is transition. We go from one stage to another, from one state of being to another, from one place to another. Growth is evolution.

Growth can be smooth or rough, slow or sudden. If you examine your life closely, you will discover you have undergone many stages of growths, of transitions -- some of them may have been smooth, and quite a number of them may have been sudden.

When you explore your life's different growth or transition events deeply and closely, you will discover these events have played vital roles in shaping you – your beliefs, your outlook, your values.

<u>Monday</u>: Make a list of ten growth or transition events before you were thirteen. Choose one event and write about it for ten to fifteen minutes.

<u>Tuesday</u>: Make a list of ten growth or transition events during your teenage years. Choose one event and write about it for ten to fifteen minutes.

<u>Wednesday</u>: Make a list of ten growth or transition events when you were a young adult, eighteen to twenty-nine years old. Choose one event and write about it for ten to fifteen minutes.

<u>Thursday</u>: Make a list of ten growth or transition events when you married or when you were between thirty to forty

years old. Choose one event and write about it for ten to fifteen minutes. If you are not married or you have not turned thirty yet, then make a list of ten growth or transition events you want to happen when you marry or turn thirty. Choose one event and write about it for ten to fifteen minutes.

Friday: Make a list of ten growth or transition events from the time you turned forty-one up to now. Choose one event and write about it for ten to fifteen minutes. If you are still to turn forty-one, then make a list of ten growth and transitions events you want to happen when you do turn forty-one. Choose one event and write about it for ten to fifteen minutes.

10 growth or transition events between 30 and 40 years old

1. Moving back to Florida
2. Being a single mom
3. Reconciliation with my son's father
4. My father's illness (cancer)
5. My father's death
6. My mom's cancer returning and going into remission
7. My mom's new boyfriend
8. Trying to contact my family for history
9. Moving in with my son's father
10. Becoming a published writer

When I was 31, I went through the most traumatic time of my entire life. My father had end-stage lung cancer and committed suicide. When I heard the news, I was at work. I knew he had died beforehand, though. I felt the chill. The feeling I used to get when he was sick and didn't yet know it. I felt it throughout my bones, and this was much worse than anything I could have imagined. I can remember everything about that day, especially when my mother took us in her arms and said, "Listen to me—he took his own life."

The hardest part of my grief has been the non-resolution of it. There are always times when I sink back into depression and cry, and wonder and ask questions and hate him for doing what he did. I don't think it will ever be fully resolved, because I loved my dad so much. I still do. I just have too many questions that will never be answered.

I grew up fast when I realized Dad wouldn't be here to talk to. I have regrets, guilt, and issues galore. Journaling my grief and fears has helped me grow into a stronger woman, a better mother, and someone who can help others through grief.

My dad dying has given me patience, insight and the ability to love more openly than I ever have. It took me a while to find these gifts. Growing like this—well, I consider them all gifts from my father. I will always miss him.

Copyright © 2003 by Dawn M. Coder

# Week Fifty: Heroes

Children are impressionable. They see something on television, they will remember it for a long time. They hear something, and they will repeat it word for word.

During formative years, a child begins to look up to adults – he or she tends to imitate actions, words and even the appearance of adults. It is this stage that a child begins to idolize an adult.

Children, and even adults, often idolize movie stars. Advertisers take advantage of this – they sign on movie stars to endorse their products (clothes, food, shampoo). If a child sees her favorite movie star endorsing a particular shampoo, she might ask her mother to buy that shampoo next time she goes to the grocery.

Everywhere we look, we will observe someone idolizing another person, whether consciously or unconsciously. While you were growing up, who were your idols? At school, who was the teacher you most admired? When you were getting ready to go to college, who or what propelled you to pursue a particular career path?

Monday: What is the first thing that comes to your mind when you hear the word "hero"? Write about it for ten minutes.

Tuesday: If you were a superhero, who would you be? Write for ten minutes.

Wednesday: Create your own hero. What characteristics does your hero possess? Spend fifteen to twenty minutes creating your hero.

<u>Thursday</u>: For fifteen minutes, write about your earliest memory when you admired or idolized someone.

<u>Friday</u>: Who is your personal hero or idol? Write him or her a letter.

My hero is, and always will be, my father.

Dear Dad,

Wow—this has been a bad night for memories.

I was cleaning out some files and papers, and going through some boxes of stuff and I came across so many things from you.

Cards you made for me. Cards you made for me from my little baby. Pictures galore. And the tape you made right before you shot yourself.

Hasn't been a good night. I've cried more tonight than I have in a long time. I guess because that dreaded anniversary of death is coming up soon. I am debating whether or not to take the day off from work. First off, I have no more personal time to take, and it may keep my mind off of it. However, if it DOESN'T keep my mind off it, I will be crying on and off all day, which isn't good for me being in health care patient services. So I don't know. Dad, I know you'd want me to go to work; but I think I just need a day to cry. I haven't had one in a long time.

A suicide dies only one death; the survivors die a thousand times trying to figure out why. And though I do know why, I still have too many questions that will never be answered. I'll have to wait 'til I see you in heaven to ask you. Did you realize any of

164

this? Did you think about how it would affect those of us left behind?

My son still remembers you, you know. He sees you, talks to you. Does it freak me out? Yeah... a bit... but it also gives me peace to know you're watching out for him.

Just wish that you were here to talk with; there are so many political things going on that we could really get into. I need to ask you advice. To laugh with you would bring joy to my broken heart. To confide in you again about certain things that happened. I miss you and it really is hard. I knew it would be hard when you died, but I didn't know that it would be like this. When you died by your own hand, my life changed forever. I lost you, my hero.

No matter what, though, I will always look up to you. Now I'll just have to look a little further into the sky.

I love you,

Dawn

Copyright © 2003 by Dawn M. Coder

## Week Fifty-One: Self-Awareness

A simple "Who am I?" can perhaps spurn you into a deeper and more meaningful exploration of yourself. You may discover many things about you and gain insights in the process

When you understand yourself fully – how your mind and heart work – you will then be able to create a masterpiece from words. Your words will have more texture, more flavor, more truth. You will be able to write something breathing with life.

And you will write with honesty. It all begins within you.

Monday: What or who has contributed to your sense of being? Write about it for ten minutes.

Tuesday: Freewrite for five minutes on each prompt:

- Beginning today, I will...
- One of the mistakes I made in the past was _____ and from that mistake, I learned...
- One of my strengths is...

Wednesday: Which of your childhood ambitions, dreams and hopes do you still carry with you? Why have you not let go of them? Write for fifteen minutes.

Thursday: Explore the reasons you continue to hold the beliefs and values you have today. Do this for ten to fifteen minutes.

Friday: If someone were to write a script or book about your life, what would the ending be?

# Week Fifty-Two: Goals

In management, there are three kinds of goals: strategic, tactical and operational. Briefly, strategic goals are broad or general targets; tactical goals and operational goals are measurable targets, with the latter being more specific than the former. Operational goals are set in very concrete and measurable terms in order to achieve tactical goals.

For example, your strategic goal is "to finish a 300-page novel within one year." Your tactical goal is "to write on a regular basis in the next ten or eleven months," and your operational goal is "to write at least three hundred words every day." Imagine that one page is equivalent to three hundred words. If you write three hundred words every day, you will have three hundred pages in less than nine months, with time to spare to edit your work or catch up with writing in case you skip writing some days. In order to achieve your strategic goal, you must commit to doing you operational goal. There is no other way. Your 300-page novel will not materialize at the end of one year if you does not give yourself smaller and more doable goals.

Many writers do not achieve their goals not because the goals they set are impossible to achieve but because they fail to set the smaller goals – the tactical and operational goals.

This week is the final week. If you have followed this book religiously for the past fifty-one weeks, then you have a pile of creative pieces you can go over and over. For your last Weekly Writes activity, you will be setting goals. During the next five days, set five different strategic goals. They can be goals you want to achieve for yourself, your family or your writing career.

After creating your strategic goals, set tactical and operational goals for each. What concrete steps can and will you take in order to achieve your strategic goals?

Keep your list of goals and remember to refer to it regularly. Work on achieving them. You have concrete steps to take in order to realize them.

Thank you for writing with me for fifty-two weeks, and congratulations on achieving the goals you are and will be setting for yourself.

I have one goal for one day this week for my future writing endeavor.

Strategic goal: To write an article on Post-Traumatic Stress Disorder within two months, for publication.

Tactical goal: Researching for two weeks; note-taking; writing first and second drafts (more, if needed).

Operational Goal: To spend at least one hour a day, possibly two if time allows, on the above goals of research, note-taking, writing the drafts, and interviews.

Concrete steps I need to take: Aside from research and note taking, I need to contact two of my friends who also suffer from PTSD and ask if they would consent to a minor interview for my article. I need to go back to my older journals and check when I started exhibiting symptoms of PTSD and write that into my article. I also need to do some research in the current version of Writers' Market, and online sources, to see who would be willing to accept a query letter regarding this topic.

# 100 Writing Sparks

In May 2003, I created **WriteSparks!™,** a software that generates writing prompts. As of February 2004, there are 15 random generators in the program: First Line, Cliché Starter, Mixed Metaphors, Mixed Proverbs, Random Story Words, What If Story, Quick Prompts, Character Profiles, Silly Paragraphs, Mixed Personifications, Tabloid Stories Sparkers, Poetic Lines, Quick Plots, Poetry-To-Go, and Quick Character Sparks. Combined, these generators can create over 10,000,000 possibilities and story starters.

You can download a free copy of **WriteSparks!™ Lite** from http://writesparks.com. The software is PC-based (it won't run on a Mac). The only requirements are Windows 95/98/ME/2000/XP and Internet Explorer version 4.0 or higher.

Below are 100 prompts generated by 4 of the 15 generators in **WriteSparks!™**. Use them to jumpstart your writing.

### 25 Mixed Metaphors

1. a spoonful of gold

2. a cage of hunger

3. a saddle of justice

4. a suit of firmness

5. a prison of laughter

6. an oasis of freedom

7. a flock of sacrifice

8. an ocean of light

9. an umbrella of hope

10. a plate of despair

11. an inch of antipathy

12. a ladder of hope

13. a chimney of sadness

14. a gallon of fear

15. a profile of brevity

16. a crate of yearning

17. a window of eloquence

18. a chapter of firmness

19. a whirlwind of solace

20. a sprinkle of chance

21. a cup of tolerance

22. a string of patience

23. a garden of convenience

24. a plate of thunder

25. a bowl of pity

## 25 Mixed Personifications

1. The music whistles as the meadow howls.

2. The daisy weeps as the valley dies.

3. Anger races as sorrow waits.

4. Sorrow speaks as the mountain wonders.

5. The daisy breathes as silence shouts.

6.  The mirror moans as dawn remembers.

7.  The meadow aches as pain speaks.

8.  Apathy charms as curiosity hums.

9.  Love breathes as the star yawns.

10.  Joy returns as the distance murmurs.

11.  The sun whimpers as the forest aches.

12.  Hope pulsates as the wave mumbles.

13.  Grief falters as love vibrates.

14.  The sea tarries as the distance moves.

15.  Apathy dies as hope remembers.

16.  Hope darts as the river howls.

17.  The star feigns as darkness sobs.

18.  The mirror shouts as chaos remembers.

19.  Sorrow withdraws as darkness beseeches.

20.  The shore fumes as the wave giggles.

21.  Passion aches as joy beats.

22.  The ocean tingles as the river croons.

23.  Darkness falters as chaos growls.

24.  The river shrieks as the space trembles.

25.  The star croons as the wave hedges.

## *20 Quick Prompts*

1.  Write about an item in your room that you do not use anymore.

2. Write about the sound of frustration.

3. Write about anticipation.

4. Write about what makes you cry.

5. Write about something that makes you nervous.

6. Write about the taste of isolation.

7. Write about what you see when you look in the mirror.

8. Write about a disastrous date.

9. Write about how you deal with fear.

10. Write about the last time you pampered yourself.

11. Write about your evening 'ritual.'

12. Write about one of your irritating or annoying habits.

13. Write a tall tale.

14. Write about the scent of perfection.

15. Write about a cheap item you once bought.

16. Write about an expensive item you once bought.

17. Write about the five things that cheer you up.

18. Write about the texture of darkness.

19. Write about the scent of rejection.

20. Write about what you would say to an uninvited guest.

## 30 Mixed Proverbs

1. Every bird seldom knocks twice.

2. A guilty conscience conquers all.

3. A rolling stone savors the first fill.

4. Death is known by his note.

5. He whose belly is full is blind.

6. Curiosity may sometimes hit the mark.

7. Abundance, like want, is better than a fat judgment.

8. Necessity travels fast.

9. A blind man is the mirror of the soul.

10. Cabbage twice cooked will find a way.

11. A good conscience catches no mice.

12. Necessity is worse than death itself.

13. The female of the species turneth away wrath.

14. Bad news wears away the stone.

15. Diligence crowns the work.

16. Experience is better than nothing.

17. Death breeds contempt.

18. A creaking cart is the mother of invention.

19. The first step makes a good ending.

20. Faith breaks the camel's back.

21. A piece of churchyard is his castle.

22. A guilty conscience is better than nothing.

23. Lightning covers a multitude of sins.

24. An open door is a great healer.

25. Discretion can serve two masters.

26. Silence never bites.

27. The back door is the great leveler.

28. Anger carries its dower in its face.

29. The covetous will clutch at a straw.

30. A good beginning is stronger than love.

# Contributors

**Angel,** soultrainchick (*soultrainchick@yahoo.com*), lives independently as a banker and writes merely for passion. She is currently enrolled in an MBA program at the De La Salle University in the Philippines. She dreams of getting a book published.

**Dawn M. Coder** (*waterfall34@att.net*) is a 34-year-old published writer and mom to a four-year-old boy. She teaches a class on Grief Journaling for Inspired2Write.

**Dayday, Tadz** (*ramontesa@zwallet.com*) works as an assistant manager in a rural bank in the Philippines. After work, she teaches at two local schools. She is a CPA and hopes to someday write something that would end up in print.

**Karen A. Izzard** (*www.weblinkcreations.com*) is a web developer and aspiring author.

**Greg Jones** (*http://home.earthlink.net/~jonesusc/*) says, "I'm a frustrated writer. Four children, a wife and a challenging job frequently leave me befuddled. I write my e-mail newsletter, Through One Man's Eyes, to share that befuddlement with my readers."

**Reiji Kanzaki** (*Reiji_8@hotmail.com*) considers himself a novice writer. He is a computer science sophomore in San Sebastian College (Manila, Philippines). "I write short stories, poems and hope to create my own role-playing game (RPG) someday. I spend my leisure time writing and playing computer or console (PS2, Xbox) games, especially RPGs (like the Final Fantasy series)."

**Melissa Konefal** (*Mellybutterfly7@earthlink.net*) is 27 and a graduate of CCSU in Connecticut. She enjoys writing short fiction, poetry, and essays and has a homepage at http://www.geocities.com/mellyk21.

**Patricia MacQueen** (*trishmacqueen@hotmail.com*) is a freelance artist, author, columnist, book illustrator and e-newspaper publisher. Trish is a grandmother of three, mother of two and a woman who is living her dream and loving it. Visit "The Shoppe," Trish's studio, gallery and office at http://www.trishmacqueen.theshoppe.com.

**Ginger Redman-McConnell** (*vmcougar@comcast.net*) lives near Nashville, TN. She began keeping a journal when a friend gave her a diary with a lock as a child.

**Sarah E. Miller** (*ReadyWriter52@aol.com*) works part time at the local library and is learning to write. She enjoys writing short stories and poetry.

**Kim Peterson** (*petersk@bethelcollege.edu*) teaches writing, journalism, communication and English courses at Bethel College. Her interests include creative writing, nonfiction articles and writing for children and young adults.

**Resmi Shaji** (*resmi_shaji@rediffmail.com*) is a freelance writer based in Kerala, India with several published works in national magazines, Web sites and newsletters. Visit her at http://travel.to/resmicreations.

**Andrea K. Tompkins** (*kmulhern@epix.net*) was born and raised in Germany, and has been living in the US since 1993. She wrote previously for a small Children's Magazine (WEE Magazine) in Allentown, PA.

**Jennifer VanSchoyck** (*witchwritermom@aol.com*) is a single mom of three under three. She is a freelance writer, editor and is currently working on a young adult novel.

**Billie A. Williams** (*billie@billiewilliams.com*) is author of Death by Candlelight and Fire at Thunder Ridge (Wings ePress, Inc.), Tung Umolomo (Publish America) and Writing Wide (Filbert Publishing, September 2003). Her articles, short stories, poetry and flash fiction have been published in various online and offline media. Web site:
http://www.billiewilliams.com

# About the Author

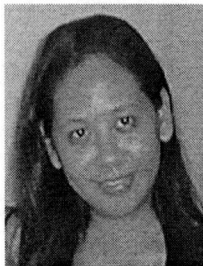

Shery Ma Belle Arrieta is founder of The e-Writer's Place (ewritersplace.com), developer of e-mail courses (writingbliss.com) and creator of WriteSparks!(tm) software (writesparks.com).

She is a contributor in Moira Allen's WRITING.COM: Creative Internet Strategies to Advance Your Writing Career (2nd ed.) and her story appears in the anthology, A Cup of Comfort for Inspiration.

She and her business partner David Russ own and run several sites including blog.forwriters.org, TimeWithKids.com, ScatterMall.com and CreativeWritingPrompts. Shery works full-time from her home in Laguna, Philippines.

## About Weekly Writes:

It began as a wildly popular e-mail course taken by thousands of writers worldwide. Today it's totally revised and updated, available for the first time in print.

Inside these pages you'll find 52 weeks... 12 solid months... of provocative writing prompts, unparalleled inspiration, and everything you need to create one of the most comprehensive journals of your writing career.

Daily writing prompts combined with vivid written examples by an eclectic group of dedicated writers will make each "assignment" a breeze.

Weekly Writes is designed to help both beginning and seasoned writers (re)discover the joy of writing, of putting pen to paper.

## Readers Say:

"This is...my kind of book. If you're ready to take creative risks, try new genres, and let someone light your imagination on fire, this book is for you." - Jenna Glatzer, bestselling author of Outwitting Writer's Block

"Prepare to have your imagination turned inside out." – Susie Michelle Cortright, founder of the award-winning Momscape.com

"The sixth grade gifted learners in the Writing Center I created used many of the prompts for their creative writing journals. My students loved the prompts!" - Cheryl McCullough, GT Programs Specialist, Fairfax County Public Schools

"Your book is wonderful. It is to writing what stretches are to an athlete before she goes into competition, what the w_____ _____ _____'s before they play the concert, or what playing scales _____ _____ _____ cital." – Sue Wagstaff, workshop instructor and auth_____

## Meet The Au_____

Shery Ma Belle Arrieta is found_____ _____ _____ _____ Place (ewritersplace.com), developer of e-mail courses (writingbliss.com) and creator of WriteSparks!(tm) software (writesparks.com).

ISBN: 0-9710796-7-6  $11.95

51195>

9 780971 079670

Filbert
Publishing